Effective Methods of Church Growth

Effective Methods of Church Growth

Growing the church by growing the Sunday School

Andy Anderson
with
Linda Lawson

BROADMAN PRESS
Nashville, Tennessee

To Eleanor who shares in all that I do:

She is my love, my friend, my partner, my keeper of the home during my long absences.

Her children depend on her wisdom; her grandchildren adore her sense of humor; total strangers confide in her; and her husband has found a "virtuous wife whose worth is far above rubies."

Thanks, honey.

—Andy Anderson

© Copyright 1985 • Broadman Press
All rights reserved
4232-37
ISBN: 0-8054-3237-X

Dewey Decimal Classification:
Subject Heading: CHURCH GROWTH
Library of Congress Catalog Card Number: 85-7873
Printed in the United States of America

Library of Congress Cataloging in Publication Data

Anderson, Andy, 1927-
   Effective methods of church growth.

   1. Church growth. 2. Sunday-schools. I. Lawson, Linda, 1945-   . II. Title.
BV652.25.A53   1985   254'.5   85-7873
ISBN 0-8054-3237-X

Foreword

This book is clear, straightforward, direct, and practical. Andy Anderson has pulled from his years as a pastor and added his vast experiences as a growth specialist for the Sunday School Department of the Sunday School Board to give us a book that deserves the attention of every church no matter what size or complexion over this nation.

I am deeply grateful for what Andy has done for all of us by giving us this resource. It should be at the side of every leader who believes in carrying out the Great Commission. The material in this book will help all of us accomplish the task more effectively.

Andy Anderson is probably best known for ACTION and the Sunday School Growth Spiral. This book tells how to accomplish our task in practical, tried, and true ways. There is help here for the pastor, minister of education, other staff members, and the Sunday School directors and teachers. I enthusiastically recommend this book.

HARRY PILAND, *Director*
Sunday School Department
Sunday School Board

Introduction

I spend a lot of my time in airports, hotels, and restaurants as I travel thousands of miles each year working with pastors and other church leaders committed to reaching people for Christ and leading their churches to grow. Wherever I go, I encounter people with needs, needs that could be met by a caring congregation of Christians, an opportunity to study God's Word, and an encounter with Jesus Christ.

One afternoon in California, I returned to my hotel room after lunch, planning to take a thirty-minute nap before the next session of a growth conference began. Instead, a maid from the hotel was cleaning my room and I encountered in her a woman who desperately needed someone just to listen.

On a Friday afternoon, I sat down in an airport waiting room next to a tired salesman who had been on the road for three weeks. Getting home for the weekend was the major concern of this fortyish man in a rumpled brown suit.

Across the room an attractive but worried-looking woman waited anxiously to put her daughter, about ten years old, on the plane for a cross-country flight to visit her father.

In a busy restaurant at lunchtime a young couple argued, voices low and tense, oblivious to the crowd around them.

Outside a downtown hotel an old man sat alone, waiting for night to fall when he would sleep—not inside the walls of the hotel but on the bench where he sat.

In the United States today, 120 million people do not attend any church. These are people who need to be involved in studying

God's Word and in relationships with Christian people. These are people who need to know Jesus Christ as their Savior.

These 120 million people may seem like faceless numbers when considered collectively. However, we need to see them and care about them as individual human beings. This happens as Christian people look for the unchurched persons around them and invest their lives in listening, witnessing, ministering, and discipling.

Imagine what could happen if every Southern Baptist pastor committed himself to spending time each day enrolling people in Bible study. Some could enroll one person each month or each week; others, one person each day. Then imagine that Sunday School directors, outreach leaders, teachers, and members decided to put their concern into action through personal visitation, witnessing, and enrolling people in Bible study. Sunday School departments, classes, and members would set regular goals for growth and develop strategies for reaching the goals.

If people in thousands of churches began actively and systematically enrolling people in Bible study, there would no longer be 120 million unchurched persons in America. As literally millions of previously unchurched people began participating in weekly Bible study, their lives would be changed as they moved from a study of God's Word to a personal knowledge of the Eternal Word.

As people are reached, more Christians will catch a vision of what it means to be on a bold mission for Jesus Christ, carrying out in the last days of the twentieth century the Great Commission that He gave us almost two thousand years ago.

ANDY ANDERSON

Contents

1

The Sunday School and Church Growth

I became a student of church growth in 1946 at the age of nineteen when I accepted my first pastorate. I have been involved ever since in reaching people for Christ and helping churches grow. The things I share with you in this book are the things I have done alongside the members in the churches where I have served. I know they have worked because I have participated in the doing of them. Not everything I have attempted has succeeded. When something did fail, I have tried to examine the experience and learn from it. I have tried to carefully evaluate the successes in order to identify principles for reaching people, developing believers, and growing churches.

As pastor of Riverside Baptist Church, Fort Myers, Florida, I began using the concept of enrolling people in Sunday School anywhere, anytime. This open enrollment concept, ACTION, became a phenomenal vehicle for reaching people for Christ, for involvement in Bible study, and for church membership.

In 1975 I was asked to become a church growth specialist for the Southern Baptist Sunday School Board in Nashville, Tennessee, and travel nationwide helping churches grow. My church growth portfolio has included three interrelated Sunday School growth projects.

First is the ACTION Sunday School Enrollment Plan, which combines the concept of enrolling people in Sunday School whenever and wherever they are encountered and agree to be enrolled, along with aggressive church strategies in setting enrollment goals and working to achieve them.

Second is the Sunday School Growth Spiral, a balanced concept of growth in which churches set enrollment goals and support these goals through starting new units and training sufficient workers. Quality Bible study is emphasized through establishing weekly workers' meetings and urging workers to participate in regular training. Outreach is emphasized through weekly visitation. As a balanced program is developed, enrollment and attendance increase along with offerings and worship attendance. As lost persons encounter the Word of God and are loved and ministered to through Sunday School classes, many become Christians.

Third is the Sunday School Super Spiral, an accelerated church growth plan, using ACTION and the Growth Spiral, in which participating churches of all sizes are experiencing phenomenal results. For example, one of the smallest churches to enter the Super Spiral is Whispering Lakes Community Church, Ontario, California, which had 19 members. After eighteen months in the program, enrollment was 346 and average attendance, 160. At the other end of the spectrum, First Baptist Church, Dallas, Texas, has been the largest participating church with 9,762 enrolled in Sunday School. In nine months, enrollment had climbed to 10,902.

GROWTH THROUGH THE SUNDAY SCHOOL

My conviction that the most important thing a church should be doing is to give priority to growth through the Sunday School has been borne out countless times as I have observed and worked with churches of all sizes and kinds in every part of America. I know it is true because I have seen it happen over and over again. More churches have been established through Sunday Schools than in any other way. More people have been reached for salvation through Sunday Schools than any other way. More people have been taught the Bible in Sunday Schools than in any other way. More people have been discipled for Christ through Sunday School than in any other way. I have never known a Southern Baptist church that was not grown through the Sunday School.

This conviction was strengthened several years ago when I

asked one of America's great pastors what made it possible for him to preach to more than eight thousand persons each Sunday. "My Sunday School teachers bring them to church," he answered.

I immediately inquired as to whether many came instead to hear him preach. "No," he repeated. "They attend on Sunday mornings because the Sunday School workers bring them to Sunday School. I believe a pastor may have an ego problem who believes people attend on Sunday mornings primarily to hear him preach."

I believe this man of God was correct in his assessment. While some people do attend only the Sunday morning worship service, most attend Sunday School first. A related truth is that while the church gathers to worship, the church functions through the Sunday School. The objective of a church is to reach lost people for Christ and church membership, involving them in discipleship and service. We are to reach and win people. We are also to baptize and disciple them. Through the Sunday School, workers and members enroll unsaved people, pray for them, minister to their needs, and encourage their attendance in the classroom where the Bible is read, studied, and applied. When a lost person is exposed to God's Word, the Holy Spirit brings a conviction of sin and produces the conversion experience. The church functions through the Sunday School, small groups of people meeting together to study God's Word and minister to one another. The church also grows through the Sunday School.

The objective of the Sunday School is reaching lost people for Jesus Christ and meaningful church membership. These two go together. The purpose of the church is not only reaching lost people for Jesus Christ *but also* reaching them for meaningful church membership which includes discipleship and service. This includes both parts of the Great Commission, Matthew 28:19-20. We are to reach and win them, but we are also to baptize and disciple them.

In order for this process to occur, Sunday School teachers must be willing to seek and to rely upon the leadership of the Holy Spirit. The teacher's responsibility is to expose the unregenerate person to the Bible, then allow God to perform the miracle of salvation.

MAINTENANCE OR GROWTH?

The second most important thing I have learned from the last eight years of working with thousands of churches is that church growth is not a matter of *how much* we do. It is *what* we do.

For example, on Sunday mornings when you review your church calendar of activities for the next week, you will probably discover that at least one church-sponsored activity is going on every night. We are busy people. But what are we busy about? Look again at the activities. Chances are that most, if not all, of the activities have to do with *maintaining* the church. Few, if any, are geared toward growing the church. Maintaining the fellowship and the programs of the church is important. But if all actions and activities are geared toward maintenance, then certainly growth will not take place. It is not *how much* we do that counts but *what* we do that produces growth in the church.

For example, here are six activities that need to be happening on a continual basis if a church is to be growth oriented rather than exclusively maintenance oriented.

1. *Greet people who attend.* This seems so obvious, yet it fails to happen in many churches. When a person attends the Kiwanis Club or Lions Club, he may be treated like a millionaire. But at church the same person may be ignored. This often starts in the church parking lot. Members should be assigned to parking lots to assist people in parking, to welcome them, and to help them know where they need to go. Others should be assigned to the hallways. Guests should be greeted. Members should be welcomed as well. This is how an initial spirit of love, concern, and care is created. People begin to feel that their presence makes a difference and that they are appreciated.

2. *Introduce, welcome, register, and enroll all visitors.* Complete records on those who visit are absolutely vital so that personal follow-up can take place. Every guest should be offered the opportunity to enroll in Bible study.

3. *Focus attention on growth.* Members must be constantly kept aware of the priority of growth and of reaching people. Announcements, prayers, items in the church bulletin and newsletter, bulletin boards, and sermons should highlight the importance of reaching people for Christ, establishing the church's growth goals, and making progress toward achieving the goals.

4. *Emphasize the importance of locating and contacting prospects.* Prospects are the resource for enrolling people in Bible study. A church cannot grow without prospects. Members must be kept conscious of the importance of seeing and identifying prospects wherever they go.

5. *Express public appreciation for those who work at growth.* Say thank you to those who participate in visitation. List their names in the bulletin or newsletter. When a person is enrolled in Sunday School, joins the church, or makes a profession of faith, the person or persons who were instrumental in his or her becoming involved should be identified.

6. *Ask for and expect God's blessings on growth activities.* Great emphasis is given in most churches to praying for the crisis needs of members. This is vitally important. At the same time, prayer for growth activities such as weekly visitation should be emphasized. Those who go out should be prayed for by name. Those who will be visited should be prayed for by name. God will bless our efforts if we allow him to lead us and we ask for his blessings.

FOUR TYPES OF CHURCH GROWTH

Because the term *church growth* means different things to different people, it is important to note that there are four types of church growth. (See p. 21.) First, there is *internal growth*, growth in grace. Internal growth takes place when the church is edified and when Christians grow more like the Master. Second is *numerical growth*, when a church experiences increases in Sunday School and worship attendance, offerings, and baptisms. This is *new work growth*, starting a new church in another community. Fourth is *interlocking growth*, starting a new congregation across a significant cultural barrier such as language or race. The new congregation may meet in the same church building but function as a separate church in order to reach and minister to a particular group.

Each of these types of growth is important for balance if we wish to carry out the full commission of our Lord Jesus Christ. On the one hand, it is impossible to emphasize internal growth or making disciples if members are not led to practice their discipleship by reaching people. On the other hand, as the church experiences numerical growth, it is vital that new Christians and new members experience meaningful Bible study and the training that enables them to grow and mature in their faith.

ASSUMPTIONS ABOUT GROWTH

In order for a church to be in a position to grow, leaders and members must accept these seven assumptions about growth.

1. *Church growth is the will of God.* This takes us back to the Great Commission. Jesus told us to go everywhere and reach all people. If we are going to live out this commandment, we are going to reach people. Christ also emphasized the importance of the church, calling it His bride. If we are going to involve people in churches, then churches are going to grow. And yet there are many persons in churches who do not want to see their church grow. Some fear losing power and influence if more people are brought into the church. Others like their class or department the way it is and don't want new people coming in. Others fear change—a new building, new program, new ways of doing things. Others fear that a commitment to reaching people will bring undesirables into the church.

2. *Church growth principles apply in all places, at all times, and to all churches.* In other words, every church can grow. Churches do have different levels of potential for growth, but every church can grow.

3. *Hindrances to church growth can be identified, isolated, and overcome.* The hindrance may be the pastor or a key leader. It may be money or a lack of space. The hindrance may be a bad experience that happened in the past. It can be identified. Once it is identified, it can be isolated. Then it should be put in the hands of God.

4. *Planning is essential to church growth.* A church that does not plan to grow will not grow at its level of potential.

5. *Leadership is the key to church growth.* The pastor is the primary key to church growth. If he does not want the church to grow, it will not grow. On the other hand, the pastor cannot grow a church by himself. The support and commitment of key leaders is a necessity.

6. *The Holy Spirit is the dynamic of church growth.* This is foundational. God's leadership in every plan and every action must be sought and followed.

7. *Growth is the sign of a healthy church.* The first ingredient in a quality church is reaching the lost.

MONITOR SPIRITUAL HEALTH

It is vital that leaders regularly inventory the spiritual health of their church. The following five tests are important indicators to help a church determine if it is in a healthy, sick, or dying condition.

A negative finding on one of the five tests may not mean serious problems exist. Exceptions can be found in each of the five areas. However, because the five tests measure interrelated facets of church life, a church that is healthy in one area is more likely to also be healthy in the other four. Likewise, where a dying condition is indicated in one area, sick or dying indicators in the other four areas frequently follow.

Test #1—Sunday School Enrollment. If a church has experienced a net increase in Sunday School enrollment in the past twelve months, a healthy condition is indicated. If enrollment has remained static over the past year, the church may be sick. If the Sunday School enrollment has declined, the church may be dying.

Test #2—Tenure of Church Members. Survey the entire church membership roll, noting how long each person has been a member. Find the midway point in tenure of membership. If one-half of the church members have belonged to the church ten years or less, indicating new growth has taken place, the church is in a healthy condition. However, if one-half of the members have belonged to the church between ten and twenty years, it is in a sick condition. If one-half have been members more than twenty years, indicating little new growth, the church is dying.

Test #3—Finances. A church is healthy if one-third of the church members contributes two-thirds of the income. A church is sick, however, if one-fourth of the members contributes three-fourths of the income. If one-fifth of the membership contributes four-fifths of the income, a church is dying.

Test #4—Deaths. A church's physical death ratio is determined by the number of deaths within the church family in a one-year period. If the ratio is one death per one hundred members, a healthy situation is indicated. If the ratio is between one and 2.5 deaths per one hundred members, indicating a disproportionate number of senior adults in the membership, the church may be dying. It is important to note that there may be strong exceptions to this test. A church located in a retirement community would be one. On the other extreme, a very transient membership such as a military congregation might have a much lower than average physical death ratio.

Test #5—Baptisms. A church is healthy if it baptizes more than six per 100 members. A church should be concerned if it is baptizing four or five per 100 members. But if a church is baptizing three or less per 100 members, it should pray for forgiveness and seek God's help in gaining a burden for lost people.

Once you have checked these five tests, you can probably see that one is usually dependent upon the other. For instance, if a church has a healthy gain in Sunday School enrollment, chances are it has received a number of new church members, finances are on the increase, the physical age of the membership is lower, and baptisms are increasing because more lost people have enrolled. On the other hand, if a church's Sunday School enrollment has declined, similar drops probably have also been experienced in other areas. These tests are not all-inclusive, but they can be indicators of the condition of the church.

Church growth is not automatic. A church does not grow unless it plans to grow. And even when a church plans to grow, growth will not take place in a negative atmosphere. For example, in nature, plants grow in the spring and summer. Growth takes place because the correct atmospheric conditions exist. The temperature is warm and the ground is moist. However, in the fall and winter when temperatures drop, very little growth takes place. Growth does not happen in cold temperatures. Likewise, in our churches, we need to concentrate on developing an atmosphere that is warm and conducive to growth. A growing church is one where new persons are welcomed and made to feel a part of the fellowship. A growing church is one in which meeting the needs of people is more important than the inconvenience of change that may be required to meet those needs. A growing church is one in which the Bible is taught and preached under the guidance of the Holy Spirit and people are invited to respond to God's invitation to salvation.

Seven areas of emphasis form the basis for every growing church. They also form the outline of the remainder of this book. A growing church must have:
—clear purpose
—supernatural power
—dedicated personnel
—increased participation
—quality product
—caring productivity
—specific plan.

OUR OBJECTIVE

Reaching lost people for Jesus Christ and meaningful church membership

OUR METHOD

Involving lost people in life-changing Bible study.

FOUR TYPES OF "CHURCH GROWTH"

I — INTERNAL GROWTH

is Growth in Grace. Takes place when the Church is Edified.

II — NUMERICAL GROWTH

Numerical increase of a Local Church.

III — NEW WORK GROWTH

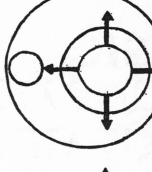

Planting a Congregation in another Community.

IV — INTERLOCKING GROWTH

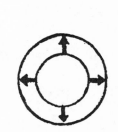

Planting a Congregation across significant Cultural Barriers.

7 BASIC ASSUMPTIONS ABOUT GROWTH

1. Church Growth is the will of God.

2. Church Growth principles apply in all places, at all times, and to all churches.

3. Growth is the sign of a healthy church.

4. Hindrances to church growth can be identified, isolated, and overcome.

5. Planning is essential to church growth.

6. Leadership is the **Key** to church growth.

7. The Holy Spirit is the Dynamic of Church Growth.

Church Health

	GREEN Healthy	CAUTION Sick	RED Dying
Sunday School	a net increase	maintenance	a net decrease
Tenure of Church Membership (½ of members)	0-9 years	10-20 years	20+ years
Finances	1/3 contribute 2/3	1/4 contribute 3/4	1/5 contribute 4/5
Physical Death Ratio (Annually)	1 per 100 members		2½ per 100 members
Baptisms	6+ per 100 members	4-5 per 100 members	3 or less per 100 members

2

A Clear Purpose

In order to be in a position to grow, church members must have a clearly focused understanding of their purpose for existence and what they should be doing to achieve their purpose.

The overarching purpose of a New Testament church where members attempt to base thoughts and actions on the Holy Scriptures must be to carry out the Great Commission, Matthew 28:19-20:

"Go, then, to all peoples everywhere and make them my disciples: baptize them in the name of the Father, the Son, and the Holy Spirit, and teach them to obey everything I have commanded you. And I will be with you always, to the end of the age" (GNB).

In the Great Commission Jesus challenges his followers, today as two thousand years ago, to emphasize three actions: (1) going; (2) evangelizing; (3) discipling. But who is the church and where can these three actions be taken to achieve the most effective results?

According to the New Testament, a church is an organism, a living organization. Generally speaking, the members of the congregation in the morning worship services do not consider themselves a group organized to carry out the Great Commission. People attend worship services for personal help and motivation for making it through another week. So, who will do the going? And where should the evangelism and discipleship take place? It is my conviction that the Sunday School is the organization, and Sunday School members and leaders are the people who will carry out the Great Commission, enabling a church to live up to its purpose.

It is through Sunday School classes and departments that most of the personal visits and contacts are made as people build relationships with others dealing with similar needs and concerns. The Sunday School fulfills the going challenge in the Great Commission.

As relationships are cultivated and needs are met in small groups and on a one-to-one basis, the Sunday School already has the organization for fulfilling the command to evangelize. More people are saved through the Sunday School than through any separate church organization for evangelism. Where churches are giving strong emphasis to enrolling lost people in Sunday morning Bible study, ministering to them and nurturing them through regular Scripture study, one-half of those who are enrolled make professions of faith within twelve months.

As people are won to Christ, their greatest need is for assistance in learning how to live a Christian life. If left on their own, many quickly lose the initial excitement about their faith and never become involved in any church. The Sunday School class is the place where discipleship happens, through teaching biblical truths and modeling the Christian life.

GOING

Is it possible to have a Sunday School class if none of the members or prospects attend on Sunday morning? The answer is no if the sole purpose of the class is to teach a lesson on Sunday mornings. The answer is yes if the teacher also sees him- or herself as a minister commissioned to meet the needs of members and prospects where they are.

The paradox is that if the teacher goes into the homes of people and ministers to their needs, some of them will come on Sunday mornings. The reason many don't come to Sunday School is that their needs are not being met. Many needs can't be met in the classroom. The concept of Sunday School must be expanded to include both teaching *and* ministering. When this has been done, whether a person attends is no longer the primary criterion for whether he can be enrolled. A person who agrees to be enrolled is a person who can be prayed for and ministered to, whether or not he attends the class sessions on Sunday morning. If the teacher is faithful in continuing to go, express concern, and minister, the day is much more likely to arrive when the person will attend. If the person is not enrolled, chances are great that the church will not have an avenue for ministry with this individual.

The Sunday School is the "going church." More visits are made by the Sunday School teachers and workers than the rest of the church. This is true because of the organization and function of the Sunday School. It is organized by small units so that ministry can be performed with individuals.

Sunday School teachers, outreach leaders, and group leaders must be trained to be visitation specialists. Their training should include doctrine, methodology, evangelism, and discipleship.

The design of the Sunday School involves weekly visitation—ministry, evangelistic and enlargement visitation. The minimum goal for people involved in visitation is at least one person from each teaching unit in the Sunday School.

The "going" part of the Great Commission is best done through the Sunday School. In Luke 14:16-24, we are told to go out into the streets and lanes of the city . . . and into the highways and hedges, and compel the people to come in that His house may be filled. God is pleased when His house is filled on Sunday morning and evening. Even though many people will give every kind of excuse imaginable and even lie to avoid going to God's house, we are still told to go out and bring them in.

Somebody may say, "I just don't have the talent to visit."

Talent is not what a person needs to obey the command to go. Faithfulness is what is required, faithfulness to go and do what God said to do and what Jesus Christ commanded. We must be willing to work at going and God will supply all our needs.

The first step in soul-winning and fulfilling God's purpose for the church is to go. In the Great Commission, the word *go* comes before preaching, teaching, and even baptizing. Fulfilling God's commandment begins with going.

EVANGELIZING

As a pastor, I became concerned that our church needed to give greater priority to evangelism. So we instituted an evangelism program that emphasized beginning with training deacons to witness. After about six months in the program, our deacons and other leaders had led many persons to make professions of faith. But as I reviewed the statistics, I was discouraged to learn that only about 18 percent of the people we had led to the Lord were baptized into the fellowship of our church. I have since learned through numerous surveys that this low percentage of baptisms is a common result of any evangelism program operated separately from other church programs. When I discovered this statistic in my church, we temporarily shut down the evangelism program to evaluate our actions. I was not willing to lead many people to the Lord but not lead them into the church. I don't believe this is scriptural.

When we restarted our evangelism program, we used the same methods, but we changed the focus. We brought evangelism into the Sunday School. First, we conducted the Sunday night witness training sessions with our Sunday School workers. Then we asked those in training to participate in Monday night visitation. The persons they visited were those who were prospects for their Sunday School class. When we channeled our evangelism efforts through the Sunday School, we began baptizing 94 percent of the persons led to the Lord instead of the earlier 18 percent. This change took place because the Sunday School class became the follow-up unit. When a separate soul-winning program is created in the church—whether it is made up of deacons, Sunday School teachers, or any other group of persons—people who are won to the Lord have no group to belong to for further teaching, nurturing, or ministry.

In addition to follow-up, there are three other advantages to evangelizing through the Sunday School. First, when a lost person becomes involved with the Word of God, the Holy Spirit is given time to speak to the person's heart and cause him to become aware of his need for salvation. Second, the person is given time and resources through the class to count the cost of becoming a Christian. He is, therefore, more likely to make a lasting, life-changing decision. Third, the lost person is surrounded with the prayers and love of fellow class members. When he makes a decision to accept Christ, he does not feel alone.

The Sunday School Evangelism Team consists of the pastor, Sunday School teachers, and Sunday School class members. (See

p. 35.) The role of the pastor on the Sunday School Evangelism Team includes leading a worship service of prayer, music, sermon, and invitation that challenges to decision and action. The pastor is also to assist members and teachers in witnessing. The Sunday School teacher has two major functions on the evangelism team: to lead a Bible lesson that God can use to touch hearts and lives, and to present the plan of salvation to lost persons in class. The class member likewise has two responsibilities: to find and bring unsaved and unenrolled persons to Sunday School and church, and to witness to the best of his/her ability. Every Christian is called to be involved in evangelism.

Who best can lead children to Christ? Who is best qualified to work with a child who has reached the age of accountability? When a child reaches that beautiful, magic moment in his life, the parent or teacher who has been working with that child week by week recognizes what is happening. That is the person to step in and lead this child to an intelligent decision for Jesus Christ.

Who is best qualified to lead a youth to Christ? His Sunday School teacher who will not only lead him to the Lord but will help him get a good start in his faith through weekly Bible study and building and maintaining a strong personal relationship with him.

Who best can lead adults to Christ? Sunday School teachers.

The Sunday School is the greatest army of dedicated evangelists in the world. They are already in touch with lost persons. Instead of leaving the Sunday School alone and creating a separate organization, we need to use the greatest organization for evangelism that God ever gave us, the Sunday School.

DISCIPLING

What is discipleship?

"Helping a new Christian understand the basis of living the Christian life," one person may answer.

Another concludes that discipleship is participation in an in-depth discipleship training program.

Both persons are correct, or partially so. Discipleship *is* helping a new Christian and training to become a more mature practitioner of the faith.

Discipleship is also teaching the basic tenets of doctrine. Discipleship is one believer encouraging another to remain faithful.

How do we carry out discipleship in a local church?

In my opinion, Bible teaching and discipleship are inextricably linked. Therefore, Sunday School workers need to be *trained* to be disciplers. Then discipleship in a church is accomplished through the Sunday School organization and Sunday School workers. To be effective, discipleship must involve the majority of persons in the church as participants with a trained network of leaders; and the Sunday School is the only organization in the church that meets these criteria.

Let us say that Mary Smith unites with the church on Sunday morning. She has become a Christian during the week when two personal evangelists from the church (Sunday School workers) visited in her home. On the Church Membership Application Card, there is no mention of joining the Sunday School. If this is the case, the church has missed its first opportunity for follow-up, to help Mary embark on a discipleship program. On the other hand, if a line on the card states: "Enroll me in Sunday School—_____ already enrolled: _____ yes; _____ no," we set into motion a discipleship program. When the new convert unites with church *and* Sunday School, she is immediately surrounded with a group of persons and a teacher who will love her, pray for her, visit her, and lead her in the Christian life.

When new people join our churches, the Sunday School leaders—properly trained—become the best disciplers we have. Church Training is designed to train disciplers. Therefore, all Sunday School leaders should actively participate in discipleship training at all times.

As persons encounter Bible truth, they need to be led to understand its meaning, apply it to their lives, and practice the application through studying, praying, ministering and witnessing. This is discipleship.

ATMOSPHERE OF GROWTH

As previously outlined in this chapter, a church is living up to the purpose for which it was created when members are involved in outreach, evangelism, and discipleship. So one way to evaluate the degree to which a church is measuring up to its purpose is to carefully measure its efforts and results in these three key dimensions. A second way to evaluate how well a church is accomplishing its purpose is to measure effectiveness in the following ten areas, distinctives which set apart churches that are creating the kind of atmosphere in which the Holy Spirit is able to work most effectively.

1. *Family atmosphere*—Growing churches, large and small, have an atmosphere of warmth which causes people to feel at home. This may be called *koinonia*. It is more than an outward show, more than the results of efforts of a good fellowship committee. This is an atmosphere produced by an *agape* love among the members—caring, compassion, concern, unity. People are drawn into this kind of atmosphere. "Where the Spirit is, there is unity." Churches which have a family atmosphere sponsor blood banks, clothing closets, transportation, help in finding jobs and housing, food for the needy. The members love and care, not only for each other but for all members of the community. New people want to be a part of this group.

2. *Growing Sunday School*—Nothing creates an atmosphere where growth can happen as much as growth itself, both numerical and spiritual growth among the members. A church can grow when Christians study, pray, visit, disciple, and minister together. The Sunday School is the best organization for carrying out the Great Commission.

3. *Heartfelt Music*—By heartfelt music, I do not mean that all music has to be foot-patting or hand-clapping rhythms or special harmonies. The music in growing churches is not all alike in style. Selections may be as familiar as "The Old Rugged Cross" and "Amazing Grace" or as stately as "Holy, Holy, Holy." But all music is played and sung with heart, with meaning. Music is intended to move the emotions and motivate the heart. This is the kind of music I find in growing churches.

4. *Trained lay evangelists/counselors*—The churches that are setting the pace in baptisms are those which are giving priority emphasis to personal soul-winning. In churches I visit that are growing, the pastor is setting the pace by modeling how to be a soul-winner. He visits every day. He takes church members with

him. As he witnesses, he demonstrates to laypersons how to win people to Christ. Trained personal evangelists in growing churches should be used to counsel those who respond to the invitation during the worship services. This helps them to grow in their ability to witness and minister and enables the pastor to continue leading the invitation.

5. *Strong Bible preaching*—It has been my privilege to hear many pastors of growing churches. With few exceptions, they are expository preachers. They change to topical or textual sermons for special occasions, but their primary method is verse-by-verse, chapter-by-chapter, book-by-book preaching.

In my first pastorate, I spent almost every week trying to find a sermon in a book which I could adapt and apply to my members. I spent hours each week thumbing through books trying to find something to preach the next Sunday. Then I learned that there can be a difference between preparing sermons and preaching the Word. I became aware that the members of my congregation were hungry for the Word of God, but I did not know how to study for this kind of preaching. It took many hours and a lot of hard work to learn new techniques of Bible study which would equip me to preach the Word to my people. I became an expositor of the Bible. I believe this is the kind of preaching that feeds the sheep.

6. *Strong visitation/contact program*—There are three ways to grow a church—visit, visit, and visit. This is the biblical plan. We are to visit in the highways, in the hedges, in the streets, and in the lanes. An effective visitation program begins with a priority followed by a plan which is activated by hard work and undergirded by prayers. But visitation is not enough. The number of people who can be visited is limited by the number of hours which can be given to this activity. In addition, contacts should be emphasized—by telephone and mail as well as personal visits. Through contacts, we can remind people of the value of Bible study and invite them to be present. Scores of postcards can be mailed each week. Sunday School attendance increases when visitation and contacts are promoted.

7. *Strong pastor*—A pastor of a growing church has discovered the following things. First, he knows who he is. Second, he knows he has received a definite call by the Holy Spirit to be a pastor. Third, he knows he has been called to pastor this specific church.

When a pastor has settled these three matters and knows he is in the center of God's will, he is in a position to be a strong, dynamic leader. I am deeply troubled by the frequency with which pastors are moving from church to church. If God were leading in all of these changes, God could be accused of hurting His church. Of course, God would not injure His church or thwart the outreach of His people. Yet growth cannot happen in an atmosphere in which a pastor is unhappy and desiring to move elsewhere. I fear too often that pressures, inadequate financial considerations, and the prestige of a larger church cause pastors to lose sight of their original call. The prophet of God does not move when trouble or discouragement arises. He does not move when the salary is not large enough. He does not move when Jezebel threatens or the brook dries up. He moves only when God issues a clear, definite call.

8. *Meaningful prayer practices*—This includes a weekly prayer service, but usually it is also more. In one church a group of intercessors meets weekly on Monday night. Another has formed several prayer groups that meet weekly. Others have twenty-four-hour-a-day prayer lines. Some have groups who pray around the clock each Saturday. In addition to these groups devoted exclusively to prayer, prayer is an important, vital part of every worship service, Sunday School class, and every meeting that is conducted in the name of the church.

9. *Leadership that helps members discover and use their spiritual gifts*—The Holy Spirit gives gifts to every Christian. Church leaders have a responsibility to help new Christians discover these gifts and give opportunities for their use.

I recall a new Christian in my last pastorate who was gifted in personal soul-winning. He had not been through courses of study or memorized Scripture verses, but he shared his testimony and invited others to receive Jesus as Savior. Almost every Sunday he brought to church one or more converts. When the invitation was given he led his friends to unite with the church. Then we discovered that Woody, a plumber by trade, was good at working around the church property. Soon he was placed on the House and Grounds Committee. Then because he could smoke fish better than anyone around, he spent much time preparing meals for class suppers. One day he came by my office and said, "Andy, I don't know what has happened. I don't have time to do soul-winning any more." I pleaded guilty. I had taken a man with a soul-winning gift and made him a cook. Church leaders, when guided by the Spirit, can help their people find and use their gifts.

These nine distinctives, then, characterize a church that is going, evangelizing, and discipling people in the name of Christ. People are busy carrying out the Great Commission. The church is living up to the clear purpose set forth by God. And it is growing.

SUNDAY SCHOOL EVANGELISM TEAM

CLASS MEMBER

FIND AND BRING LOST AND UNENROLLED PERSONS TO SUNDAY SCHOOL AND CHURCH

WITNESS TO THE BEST OF ABILITY

TEACHER

LEAD A BIBLE LESSON THAT GOD CAN USE TO TOUCH HEARTS AND LIVES

PRESENT PLAN OF SALVATION TO LOST PERSONS IN CLASS

PASTOR

LEAD A WORSHIP SERVICE OF PRAYER, MUSIC, SERMON, AND INVITATION THAT CHALLENGES TO DECISION AND ACTION

ASSIST MEMBERS AND TEACHERS IN WITNESSING

EVERY CHRISTIAN INVOLVED IN EVANGELISM

3

Supernatural Power

Church growth comes from God. When the leadership of the church becomes convinced it is the will of God that their church grow and they dedicate themselves to carrying out the Great Commission, then the atmosphere is created, the foundation is laid, and the work can begin.

God's supernatural power in the minds and hearts of church members committed to reaching people for the Lord will produce three results: (1) salvation; (2) sanctification; (3) prayer.

SALVATION

Only the supernatural power of God can produce salvation. And three basic ingredients must be present for a person to be saved. First, a person must be convicted or convinced that he is a sinner in need of forgiveness and salvation. Second, he must repent or ask God for forgiveness and salvation. Third, he must have the faith to believe that God will do what he says he can do.

One of the ministries of the Holy Spirit is to convict a person of his sin. A sinner cannot turn to God whenever he chooses. He can come to God only when the Holy Spirit draws him. Men and women and boys and girls have the power within themselves to "turn over a new leaf" or to make resolutions about making changes in their lives, but they cannot repent without the help of God.

The process of salvation sounds simple and it is simple—

"Believe on the Lord Jesus Christ, and thou shalt be saved" (Acts 16:31). And yet to understand what it means to accept God's gift of salvation and how to be saved, people need the guidance of a caring Christian witness.

The supreme mission of the church is to win souls to Jesus Christ. The very life of our churches depends upon it. However, Christians must understand not only how to witness but why. We are not to win souls just to keep our churches alive. At the same time, it is true that if our churches are alive and well, they will continue to win souls. As previously stated, I believe the best way to initiate and continue an active ministry of winning souls and ministering to needs is through the Sunday School.

In the Sunday School, every teacher and worker is a minister, not only to the persons who are members but to prospects as well. In a loving, caring atmosphere, a person is taught the Bible, visited regularly, and ministered to. If he or she is not a Christian already, efforts will be made to lead that person to a saving knowledge of Jesus Christ.

So in a church in which leaders and members are committed to carrying out the Great Commission through the supernatural power of God, the following things happen to produce salvation.

1. An organized weekly program of outreach is maintained through the Sunday School. The minimum goal of participants is one person from each preschool and children's department and one from each youth and adult class.

2. An ongoing program of witness training is conducted. All Sunday School workers are strongly urged to participate and Sunday School members encouraged to receive the training.

3. Sunday School teachers know the spiritual condition of their members and regularly seek to witness and minister.

4. The plan of salvation is presented regularly in older children's departments and youth and adult classes and departments.

5. Continual emphasis is given to the importance of enrolling and involving lost people in Sunday School. This is emphasized from the pulpit, through the Sunday School, and through church bulletins and newsletters.

6. All church members are regularly encouraged to invite and bring their lost friends to Sunday School and worship.

7. Lost persons are prayed for individually on a regular basis.

8. In each worship service, the plan of salvation is outlined briefly and simply, both orally and in writing through the church bulletin.

9. Testimonies of salvation experiences are shared regularly in Sunday School and worship services.

10. The role of Christians in sharing a witness and leading people to Christ is highlighted and affirmed on a regular basis.

SANCTIFICATION

Dictionary definitions of the word *sanctification* include the following—to make holy; to consecrate; to purify or free from sin; to give religious sanction; to entitle to reverence or respect; to make conducive to spiritual blessing.

Sanctification is not merely an outward reformation. Rather, sanctification is a total change or renovation of one's life. When we accept Jesus as our Savior, we are sanctified in spirit, body, and soul. Every aspect of our lives is changed and made better. The Scripture points out that in Christ we are new creatures. In Him, all things are made new. Sin no longer has dominion over us as born-again children of God. We dwell in Him, and He dwells in us. What a privilege it is to be partakers of a divine nature through our Lord Jesus Christ as we put off the old nature which is corrupt and put on the new nature which is like God.

Shortly after he had become a Christian, a great saint of God was complimented upon the distinctiveness and beauty of his handwriting which once had been so poor as to be almost indecipherable. "I set to work to improve it when I became a Christian," he explained. "You see, I resolved that I would make my Christianity reach into every detail of my life."

Similarly, a dentist friend of mine once remarked after being complimented on a beautiful job he had completed on a patient's bridgework: "Since I became a Christian, even my dentistry has improved."

Certainly holiness and sanctification do not come by right living and/or doing righteous acts. Neither will money buy what God has purchased for us. Jesus was perfect and therefore provided a perfect salvation. So as we trust in this perfect Savior with His perfect salvation, in the sight of God we become perfected as we yield to Him and His will for our lives.

Christians who are committed to the active process of sanctification in their own lives and to following God's leadership in seeing qualitative and quantitative growth take place in their churches will likely have a part in the fulfillment of the following processes.

1. The commitment to reaching people supersedes any inconvenience caused by the fact that the church grows. Inconveniences may include crowded rooms and parking lots, periodic changes in organization and room assignments, remodeling or congestion, and a general state of change.

2. Dual emphases on evangelism and discipleship will be carried out as leaders emphasize both reaching people for Christ and helping them grow in their faith.

3. An attitude of acceptance of all persons will pervade the congregation as members grow in their ability to see people through Christlike eyes. They will grow in living out their conviction that all persons need a Christian witness. Through outreach and evangelism efforts, personal needs will be discovered and met.

4. A commitment to quality in teaching, worship, music, ministry, and every facet of the church's programs will be carried out.

5. The church will dare to be innovative in its programming—not for the sake of being different but in order to boldly go about reaching . . . teaching . . . and baptizing.

6. The congregation will develop long- and short-range plans and goals to be efficient and effective in impacting its community with the gospel.

7. Love will pervade the congregation. Differences will be confronted directly and honestly. There will be no winners and losers. The mission of the church will be deemed more important than individual egos. Persons will not be put down for expressing their opinions. God's will will be earnestly sought in all decision making.

8. The church will gain a reputation as a congregation that is making a positive difference in the community.

PRAYER

The most important element in creating an atmosphere of growth is prayer. To be effective ministers, servants, and witnesses, Christians must be motivated by a disciplined, daily devotional life.

In the Scriptures it is reported that Jesus prayed from sundown to sunrise. David prayed morning, noon, and night. Paul prayed day and night. Jacob prayed until God touched him. Elijah prayed until God locked and unlocked heaven. The spreading of the gospel moves quickly when the saints are on their knees. It moves slowly when the saints are on their feet.

The kind of prayer that creates a positive atmosphere for growth in a church does not happen accidentally. It must begin with the leadership, for praying leaders produce praying followers. Prayer must come to be viewed by members as a priority in every facet of church life and as an absolute prerequisite to decision making and action.

For example, the gift of praying for others should be lifted up. Persons with this gift should be led to form an intercessory prayer ministry, perhaps on a twenty-four-hour basis. Requests should be channeled to this ministry and members made aware of this spiritual resource in dealing with individual and corporate concerns.

A second way to highlight the importance of prayer as a necessity for growth is to emphasize spiritual needs as well as physical needs in the midweek prayer service. Too often this important time in the life of a church is limited to praying for persons who are sick or for the families of those who have died. This is important and should not be neglected, but prayer times at church should also focus on people who are lost or have become inactive in living out their faith. Absentees, prospects, and persons who are being visited by church members should be prayed for by name and in a spirit of loving concern.

Third, prayer should be emphasized as a vital element as preparation for visitation, Sunday School lesson planning, teaching, ministering, and witnessing. Too often we emphasize the methods and mechanics of church growth without giving proper emphasis to the fuel. A twelve-cylinder Rolls Royce is no better than a one-cylinder John Deere tractor if it has no fuel. Head preparation is necessary, but heart preparation is imperative. Martin Luther said, "He who has prayed well has studied well." In our churches we must pray to reach our world for Jesus Christ. We need holy men and women to encompass the globe with prayer. Holiness alone releases spiritual energy in concern, compassion, and love.

In addition to emphasizing the priority of prayer as a church body, every church member should be encouraged to develop a daily devotional life that includes prayer. The leading weakness among Christians is the lack of a daily devotional life.

In the Old Testament, Gideon asked God for tangible evidence of his presence. God responded by sending dew to wet the fleece. A fleece comes from a dead lamb. God sent the dew after the lamb was slain and the offering consumed. Gideon's victory came after God sent the dew and Gideon was confident of God's guidance. Christians today become aware of God's presence as they accept His gift of salvation. Their awareness of His presence is renewed and their power to be His witnesses is heightened as they go to Him in prayer on a daily basis.

What kind of prayer yields the boldness and caring concern needed in a growing church?

Quantity of prayer is not the answer. Neither is selfish or legalistic prayer. What is needed is accurately summed up in James 5:16: "The effectual (quality) prayer of a righteous man (one who is right with God) availeth much (gets the job done)." Genuine prayer makes a person saintly; saintly prayer makes one holy.

When a person believes that prayer is more important than thought in preparation for living the Christian life, he will not allow anything to rob him of his daily prayer time, his appointment with God. The Christian who begins with God in the cool of the day can face the problems that may come in the heat of the day.

Nothing should rob the Christian of his prayer time. The Christian who has never learned the art of praying has never learned the art of living. God depends upon his prayers. They are the pacesetters. Without much praying there will be little true leadership. Praying is as important to living a God-pleasing life as reading the Bible. The closer one comes to God through prayer, the more he realizes the awesomeness of God's power and God's love. Strength is found in dialogue with God. The "hour of power" is the name sometimes given to a church's midweek prayer service. The desperate need of this day is not an hour of power but a lifetime of power.

However, the fact that prayer is hard work cannot be denied. Its difficulty is increased by the tendency of people to allow less important activities to take over the time designated for praying. While quantity of prayer is far less important than quality, the most common sin related to prayer is that of praying too little rather than praying too much.

As Christians seriously sort out their priorities, prayer should be the first. An active prayer life will then enhance Bible study, personal witness, daily devotions, and Christian service.

A church that can enlist sufficient praying can literally move a nation toward God. The crying need today is for members of thousands of church members to be on their knees in prayer.

Through the power of prayer, Christians invoke the supernatural power of God to lead a church in reaching people and helping them to grow in their faith. As they remain faithful to carrying out the Great Commission, they will experience growth in numbers and growth in maturity in carrying out the bold mission of Christ to go and tell.

4

Dedicated Personnel

Physical, mental, emotional, and spiritual exhaustion—burnout—is becoming an occupational hazard for pastors. A pastor can work sixteen-hour days visiting the sick, counseling persons in crisis, witnessing to the unsaved, or attending committee meetings, and still not have adequate time for sermon preparation, a personal devotional life, or private moments with his family. He becomes tired. He feels guilty about the things he doesn't have the time to do. And then he attends a church growth conference and hears the statement, "The pastor is the key to whether the church will grow." This could be the statement that pushes the pastor to the point of giving up unless he also hears and understands that a church is not likely to grow if the pastor tries to do all the work himself.

To be an effective, growth-minded leader, a pastor should give attention to three priorities: (1) enlisting and training workers; (2) motivating workers; (3) coordinating the church calendar. A side benefit to the pastor will be that not only will his church grow, but more persons will be involved in the tasks of reaching, teaching, witnessing, and ministering. By giving himself to these three priorities, the pastor will become an equipper. He will have more time to experience the abundant life promised in the Scriptures.

PASTOR'S PRIORITY #1: ENLISTING AND TRAINING WORKERS

In church growth conferences I frequently ask the question, "What should be the pastor's top priority?"

The first answer I invariably receive is "preaching the Word of God under the power of God."

The question I then ask is, "Where in the Bible is that found?"

While many pastors believe that preaching should be their top priority, I don't believe this is borne out by the model of Jesus in the Bible. Jesus was the shepherd. Every pastor is an under-shepherd. Looking closely at Jesus' life and ministry, I believe his priority was enlisting and training workers. He spent virtually every waking hour at this task. At his death and resurrection, his investment of himself in the lives of the twelve disciples and countless other followers meant that the gospel could be carried to the ends of the earth.

Enlisting workers—Most churches today lack sufficient workers for all the tasks that need to be done. I believe a major reason is the pastor's failure to be involved in enlistment. The pastor is to be an equipper of the saints. This is not intended in any way to negate or put down the importance of preaching. Any pastor who enters the pulpit unprepared is not worthy of the title of pastor. If a pastor gives top priority to enlisting and training workers, he will make the time he needs for this task because he will not allow other things to interfere.

Why should the pastor take the lead in the task of enlisting workers? The primary reason is that many persons in the church will not agree to do a job unless they are enlisted by the pastor. By virtue of his position, the pastor is in a unique place to broaden the base of his leadership. The pastor should not be the only person involved in enlistment. The minister of education, Sunday School director, Nominating Committee, and others will also be involved. But if the pastor takes the lead, the church will have the workers it needs to grow qualitatively and quantitatively. At the same time, the pastor will have the time to prepare his sermons, spend time alone with God, share his faith with the unsaved, and enjoy a personal life outside the church.

To properly enlist workers, a pastor should be aware that the Sunday School needs three kinds of workers. First is administrative workers—a general Sunday School director, department directors, division directors in a larger church. The second group is the teachers. Third is outreachers—outreach leaders, secretaries, group leaders—persons who are willing to invite people to Bible study and worship, to witness and minister. How many workers are involved in Sunday School administration, teaching, and outreach will be a major determining factor in whether growth can take place.

One worker is needed for every eight Sunday School members. A Sunday School without sufficient workers will slip from a growth mentality to a maintenance mind-set because this is all workers have the time to do. A Sunday School without sufficient workers will not be in a position to enroll more persons or start new classes or departments. If workers are surviving rather than thriving, they are less likely to participate in weekly planning or visitation. The results of an insufficient number of workers will be seen in a failure of Sunday School and worship attendance to increase. Baptisms and tithes and offerings are also not likely to increase. The number of workers is the bottom line of church work that produces growth.

Training workers—As workers are enlisted, the pastor must also be involved in training them. These persons, if properly trained, become co-ministers, representatives, extensions of the pastor's ministry. The pastor cannot meet the ministry needs of every person in the church or hire enough ministers to staff the organization.

The pastor should have three overall goals in training the workers, equipping the saints. In the first place, the pastor must teach the workers to love. Christians receive the capacity for *agape* or Christian love when they are saved. But most don't know how to demonstrate love. This is clearly evidenced in the bickering and infighting among Christians. Second, the pastor must show his workers how to care, to become involved with people, meeting their needs in a spirit of compassion. Third, a pastor must train the workers to listen. People with needs are generally not looking for people to solve their problems for them. They need someone to listen to them.

I heard of a church which trained a corps of persons they called "professional listeners." These were primarily persons who had never witnessed to an unsaved person but wanted to be involved in some form of ministry. As an experiment, the group wore buttons identifying themselves as professional listeners. Many encountered persons who needed to talk, and a few had an opportunity to share their Christian testimony. One, after listening to someone pour out his heart, had the privilege of leading that person to make a profession of faith.

A pastor who enlists a sufficient number of workers and trains them to love, care, and listen will release an army that will revolutionize the community for Jesus Christ.

In addition to training workers to love, care, and listen, more specialized training will need to be offered—basic tenets of the faith and understanding and teaching the Bible, a basic understanding of the Sunday School and how it works and specialized training in meeting the needs of various age groups. The pastor should teach the course on basic tenets of the faith, introduction to the Bible, and basic Sunday School work. If the pastor does not teach all of these courses, he should take the lead in organizing, supporting, and promoting the training process.

I personally believe the pastor is the best person to lead his people in a study of biblical and doctrinal teachings. Use the Sunday night training or worship time or Wednesday night. Contact the workers you've enlisted; encourage them to participate in the training; and give them a textbook to study at home.

To be an effective teacher, most preachers need to get rid of the pulpit. Use a music stand or something similar. Get a chalkboard and an overhead projector. Forget about preaching and *teach* your people what you believe. Take your time. When you finish the first course, begin the second and then the third. Have people enlisted to provide training in working with each age group when the first three are completed.

This kind of training will change the complexion of a church. As people begin to learn, they grow. When people grow, they are motivated. People who have never worked in the church will begin to work because they know what to do and how to do it. A major reason most churches today lack sufficient workers is that they have been invited to take jobs but never shown what to do.

When the training process is complete, have a graduation service for those who have finished the courses. Borrow caps and gowns; play "Pomp and Circumstance"; have the graduates walk down the aisle; celebrate. The church now has an adequate number of workers enlisted, one for each six to eight Sunday School members and prospects. The workers are trained and ready to go to work.

PASTOR'S PRIORITY #2: MOTIVATING WORKERS

The pastor's role in motivating the workers begins when he trains them. But the pastor must also regularly be in touch with what is happening in the Sunday School and let the workers know he is still their supporter and their leader. They need to hear this from the pastor himself. This will be a continuing source of motivation.

I believe the best time and place for the pastor to regularly motivate the Sunday School workers is during the weekly workers' meeting. Growing churches emphasize the importance of Sunday School weekly workers' meetings and the presence of all workers at these meetings to plan for the next Sunday and discuss and plan outreach and ministry. A weekly workers' meeting generates successful Sunday School work. The pastor's role is, first of all, to be present. His second task is to take five minutes at the beginning of the session to motivate the workers by challenging them to be faithful to their task and encouraging them to catch a sense of excitement in ministering to people. The rest of the session is then devoted to planning.

Let me illustrate the importance of weekly time for motivation and planning. I was born and reared on a farm in South Carolina. Mother washed in an old black washpot in the backyard. Mother would put water in the pot and build a fire under it. When the water boiled, she put in Red Devil lye and threw the clothes in the pot and stirred them with a wooden axe handle. She had Octagon soap, big bars that she used on the scrub board. She could take that axe handle, lift a piece of clothing out of the pot, get hold of it with her hands, and wring it out. Then she would hang it on the clothesline. Her clothesline ran from Dan to Beersheba, and she could hang a beautiful line of clothes. When she got the clothes hung on the line, she would get a forked pole and lift the line high above the ground. That is the purpose of the pastor's motivation time during the weekly workers' meeting: to take the sag out of the week, to pick up spirits, and to encourage continuing and increased efforts.

PASTOR'S PRIORITY #3: COORDINATING THE CHURCH CALENDAR

One important way to evaluate whether a church is in a position to grow is to look at the weekly schedule of activities. How many are maintenance oriented, activities for fellowship, training, and inspiration of church members? How many are growth oriented, designed to involve prospects, nonattenders? For many churches, weekly visitation may be the only outreach-oriented activity conducted by the church. If growth is the priority, activities must reflect this priority and the pastor must be responsible for overseeing coordination of the church calendar.

The first way to integrate outreach and growth into church activities is to lead members to see that many events planned for church members also have outreach potential. For example, prospects and inactive members should be invited to every fellowship, recreation, or social event. If a church is committed to growth, the growth mentality and commitment to reaching people must permeate everything that is done.

Second, most churches try to schedule more activities than time will allow. Rather than the church's operating on a first-come, first-served basis in scheduling activities, events should be scheduled in the context of priorities. The pastor should meet with the staff and decide what they think the work of the local church should be. This list should then be taken to the Church Council to be enlarged and refined. Then the list should be publicized to the entire church. All meetings—weekly workers' meeting, visitation, Sunday School class meetings, missions meetings, committee meetings, choir rehearsals, worship services—should be listed. When everything is listed, the pastor, staff, and Church Council should sit down and prioritize the list. This will be a difficult task. Invite input from others in sorting out the priorities. Then list the day and time for each activity, listing items in priority order. When there are no more times available, draw a line across the page and consider deleting the activity below the line. Many people will be vying for time slots, and the pastor must be willing to make the final decision when compromises cannot be worked out. If growth is the stated priority of the church, but most calendar time is devoted to fellowship among the church members, then growth is not, in fact, the priority. In the context of group discussion and setting of priorities, the pastor must be willing to make the decisions that cannot be worked out any other way.

In conclusion, a pastor committed to growth is the foundation of church growth (see p. 53). However, instead of increasing the time and work pressures on the pastor, the priority of church growth can help the pastor organize his time, give his efforts to three priorities, and result in the involvement of more persons in evangelism, outreach, and ministry.

Each winter Ringling Brothers, Barnum and Bailey Circus meets in Sarasota, Florida, their winter training quarters. Before they go out on the road each spring, they hold their first shows in Sarasota, and my family has enjoyed attending. The circus act that fascinates me most is the man who spins the plates on top of sticks. He gets several spinning and then one begins to lose momentum and starts to wobble. It will fall and break if he doesn't spin it again. Sometimes more than one is slowing down at the same time. Before long, the man is breathless, trying to keep those plates spinning.

I think many pastors feel like the man in the circus trying to keep all of the plates spinning at one time. The church has many programs, and the pastor is trying to keep them all going with little sense of priorities. A pastor's role and the church's ministries can be greatly simplified by emphasizing going, evangelizing, and discipling through the Sunday School. A pastor's role can be clarified and multiplied if he will give his time to enlisting and training workers, motivating workers, and coordinating the church calendar.

I have had many pastors who have tried this approach say their workload has been lightened significantly. At the same time, because more trained persons are involved in the work of the church, the pastor is more confident that Sunday School members and prospects are being contacted, persons who are sick and bereaved are being ministered to, needs are being met. And the pastor is not doing it all himself.

One pastor of a large church said that when he implemented these three priorities, his ministry became more organized and effective. Also, he said, when he was called to the hospital to visit someone who was critically ill, it was commonplace to encounter at the hospital a caring Sunday School teacher or member who knew about the need and came to minister. This pastor had given himself to the task of equipping the saints and had vastly multiplied the ministering resources of his congregation.

GROWTH BUILDING BLOCKS

ACCURATE RESEARCH	CONSCIOUSNESS OF LOST PEOPLE	GROWTH STRATEGY
GROWTH ATMOSPHERE	GROWTH-MINDED LEADERS	BIBLE STUDY PRIORITY
A PASTOR COMMITTED TO GROWTH		

5

Increased Participation

A church's Sunday School enrollment is its most important statistic. It is more important than Sunday School attendance, worship attendance, offerings, or even the number of baptisms. The Sunday School enrollment is the group of persons who are on the rolls and within the organizational structure to be ministered to, prayed for, and personally contacted. As their needs are met, they are more likely to also become involved in weekly Bible study. When they become involved in studying God's Word in a class where people care about them, pray for them, and minister to them, they are more likely to be open to the gospel and, at some point, to make a profession of faith and begin the journey of Christian growth. A church's Sunday School enrollment is its best evangelistic indicator.

"What if he never comes?" is the main reason given for hesitating to enroll someone in Sunday School. This is based in the belief that teaching the Bible on Sunday morning is the most important task of the Sunday School. Therefore, if a person does not come, he will not participate in Bible teaching and there is no reason for him to be on the Sunday School roll.

I believe quality Bible teaching is vitally important in Sunday School, but the most important task of the Sunday School is meeting spiritual needs, wherever and whenever they are found.

The job of the Sunday School teacher is to meet the needs of the class members, not just teach a lesson on Sunday morning. To meet spiritual needs, the teacher will need to know the members personally, whether or not they attend on Sunday mornings. The teacher will need to visit in the homes of class members, stay in

55

regular personal contact with them, plan fellowship and recreation times with them—whether or not they attend on Sunday mornings. If the teacher is faithful in building and maintaining personal relationships with class members, the time will come when a member will experience a problem or crisis and that teacher can minister and meet a need in the person's life. The Sunday School is a ministering organization. People who are enrolled can be ministered to. As their needs are met, they are more likely to become involved in weekly Bible study.

A Sunday School class could be started with a teacher and twenty persons who agreed during a survey to be enrolled in Sunday School. The teacher might spend the first week making personal contacts with the members. Sunday arrives and not one of the twenty comes to Sunday School. Should the teacher give up? The teacher should spend the Sunday School hour praying by name for each member. During the week the teacher continues visiting, telephoning, cultivating relationships. As long as the teacher is faithful at praying, ministering and meeting needs, he or she is not failing. As the members' needs are met, some will also attend. And the Sunday morning Bible-teaching facet of that class will be activated. Christianity is ministering to the needs of people. The Sunday School is a ministering organization.

Four basic steps to increasing participation in Sunday School are discovering prospects, enrolling people in Bible study, making special efforts to reach persons who are hard to reach, and seeking to involve Sunday School members who do not attend.

DISCOVERING PROSPECTS

Discovering valid prospects for Bible study is a major and continuous activity for any growing church. A valid prospect is a person not presently involved in a systematic Bible study program and for whom an address and/or telephone number are available so follow-up can be done. To be in a position to grow, a church needs (as a minimum goal) the number of prospects equal to its Sunday School enrollment.

In many churches weekly visitation is promoted and Sunday School leaders urged to participate. However, when they arrive to go out visiting, they find that the only prospects are those who have been in the file for many weeks or months. This type of visitation is very discouraging. Within a few weeks, the outreachers stop visiting and the program dies. Live, viable prospects are a necessity for a visitation program to thrive and to reach people. Before a Sunday School can organize to reach the unreached, accurate records must be developed and maintained to determine how many prospects the church has, who they are, where they are, and their ages.

Prospects are the seedbed from which growth can happen. Following are several important methods for discovering prospects. (See also "50 Ways to Find People for Sunday School.")

1. *Survey*—The church field should be divided into geographical areas. Do not canvass the entire church field at one time unless follow-up can be conducted through the Sunday School with each prospect within a reasonable time limit. After prospects are discovered, they must be cultivated. When one area has been surveyed and follow-up conducted, another area should be surveyed. In most communities, any zone can be surveyed once a year since new families are constantly moving into the area.

As an area is surveyed, the initial effort should be to enroll in Sunday School those who are willing to be enrolled. But for every person who agrees to be enrolled, many other prospects will be discovered. For example, one church enrolled 63 persons in a survey of its church field and discovered 203 prospects. After cultivating and following up on these prospects for one year, 71 of them were also enrolled in Bible study.

The most important target group among prospects is unsaved persons. The purpose of the Sunday School is evangelism, yet many churches have few unsaved persons enrolled. The best place for the unsaved is in a specific Sunday School class as an enrolled member. When that happens, a class becomes responsible to pray, to love, to minister, and to witness to that unsaved person.

2. *Unenrolled Church Members*—Every church member should be enrolled in regular Bible study through the Sunday School. However, in most churches, about one-half of all church members are not enrolled in any systematic Bible study. To discover unenrolled church members, compare the alphabetized resident

church membership roll and the Sunday School roll. Prospect cards should be prepared on each church member not enrolled in Sunday School. These should be assigned to Sunday School classes for follow-up.

3. *Inside Survey*—Ask all Sunday School workers and members of youth and adult classes to provide names of unenrolled friends and members of their families. One effective method is to distribute cards at least once a quarter in Sunday School or the worship services, asking for names, addresses, and telephone numbers of prospects. The card should also include space for the name of the person suggesting the prospect. Information on the cards should be verified and prospect cards prepared and distributed to Sunday School classes for follow-up and cultivation.

4. *Register Sunday School and Worship Visitors*—Names, addresses, and telephone numbers of all visitors must be obtained. Sunday School workers must be trained and encouraged to obtain this information. In the worship services, this may be accomplished by the distribution of cards to be collected with the offering. Another method is to register all persons in the worship service through the use of cards or books in the pew racks. Again, immediate follow-up on all prospects discovered by this method and others is vitally important.

5. *Weekly Visitation*—New prospects often can be discovered through visitation as outreachers find new residents, members of families previously known, referrals, etc. Care should be taken to obtain pertinent information on each person. Cards should be filled out and distributed to appropriate classes for follow-up and cultivation.

6. *Other Bible Study Activities*—Prospects for Sunday School may be discovered among participants in other church-sponsored activities of the church—Vacation Bible School or weektime Bible study groups meeting in homes, apartment complexes, or at the church. Names of participants in these activities need to be compared to the Sunday School rolls and prospects located and assigned to Sunday School classes for follow-up. Other family members may then also be discovered as prospects.

7. *Neighborhood Watch*—Divide the church field into neighborhoods and ask church members to observe new persons who move into the area and make personal contact with them. When

this is handled effectively and good records are maintained, the result is a perpetual census of the church field.

8. *Real Estate Sales*—In some areas it is possible to obtain the names of those who purchase real estate in the community. This is another important source for prospects.

9. *Persons in Transition*—Persons undergoing changes in their lives are often especially open to a visit or ministry from a church. A move into a community, marriage, the birth of a child, divorce, illness, death, the departure of the last child from the home—these are all transition points for personal contact and ministry.

10. *Electrical or water connections*—In some communities it is possible to obtain the names and addresses of families who apply for electrical or water hookups. This is an excellent way to learn names of families moving in. Check to see if this information can be obtained in your community.

11. *Welcome Wagon*—Many communities have some form of service to greet newcomers. These names can often be obtained on a regular basis, sometimes for a small fee.

12. *Day School, Kindergarten, Mother's Day Out, Family Life Center*—These and other services and ministries provided by a church offer a reservoir of prospects. One pastor said his church receives about ten families each year for church membership through their initial involvement with the church's kindergarten. The director of a church family life center in Oklahoma requires all persons to register when they use the facilities. The form requests information about Sunday School and church membership. When he notices persons not enrolled in Sunday School, he invites them to enroll immediately. Names of new enrollees and prospects are channeled through the church office to appropriate Sunday School classes. A Texas pastor told me the church's Mother's Day Out ministry provides one prospective family each week. "We do not offer this service just for this reason, but God gives us the opportunities," he said. "A definite system should be developed by each church to channel these prospects to the proper person. Do not lose them."

13. *Formal Invitation to Baptism*—Before a service of baptism, provide eight to ten formal invitations to each person who will be baptized. These are to be used to invite friends and family. They are available in Christian book stores or can be designed and

printed by the church. This is an important ministry to new converts who want those close to them to witness their baptism. It is also a good way to discover prospects because the friends of new converts are often not Christians.

14. *"Have a Meal on Us"*—Visitors to the church and the Sunday School should be given a card saying, "Have a Meal on Us," inviting the person to Wednesday family night supper at no cost. Records should be maintained on who is given the cards. When persons come, they should be paired at supper with members from appropriate Sunday School classes.

15. *Special Events*—Special events such as a Christmas musical or an Easter drama should be planned with outreach in mind as well as providing a meaningful experience for members. Schedule enough performances so that persons in the community can participate. Advertise the events and distribute tickets (at no cost) to assure that persons who attend will have a seat. On the evenings of the presentations, invite people to fill out a card if they want to be notified of other presentations. Some of these persons will become prospects.

16. *Telephone*—Face-to-face contact is generally the most effective method for discovering and following up on prospects, but the telephone should also be used in a coordinated effort. For example, one method would be to take the names of newcomers to the community and make initial contact by telephone. Information gained this way would eliminate some as prospects, such as persons active in another church or denomination. Also, for those who are prospects, names and approximate ages of family members could be learned. This information could be added to the records and visitation assignments given to those from the appropriate Sunday School classes. Also, after personal visits are made, follow-up by telephone can be done. One method by which many calls can be made in a short time is for a group of outreachers to gather at an office which has several phone lines. Every person has a telephone list. There may be more callers than outside lines; but each time a line becomes available, another person can make a call.

Ideas for locating prospects are endless and are limited only by failure to think creatively and outside traditional lines. As these methods are utilized, an accurate and up-to-date records system must be maintained.

A central prospect file must be established with the names, addresses, and phone numbers of all prospects. All contacts by church members should be reported and maintained in the central file. Prospect books for Sunday School classes and departments must also be maintained and coordinated with the central file. Outreachers generally should visit persons who would be in their class or department.

Many churches also find it beneficial to maintain a large map in a central location with pins showing locations of all prospects. This helps to keep before the church members the importance of visitation and the need of persons in the community to be involved in Bible study and to be reached for Christ. Also, when a member notices that a prospect lives near him, he should be encouraged to check in the church office, obtain a person's name, and make a neighborhood visit.

ENROLLING PROSPECTS

Prospects are the seedbed from which growth takes place. As prospects are visited and relationships cultivated, regular efforts should be made to enroll them in Sunday School. One of the paradoxes in many churches is that while the Sunday School enrollment is the most important figure in the church, joining the Sunday School can often be more difficult than joining the church. People may attend a Sunday School class for many weeks and never be invited to join. The first few weeks it may be assumed they are visitors, so they are not invited to become members. Then when they continue to attend, people assume they are members and do not invite them to join. In the meantime, the church may have no record of their address. No personal contact has been made by the Sunday School teacher or the pastor. No relationships are developed. No needs are discovered and no ministry takes place. One day the person may stop attending and the church will never know why he came in the first place or why he stopped attending. A soul may have been lost for God's kingdom.

In churches where enrollment has not been emphasized, three methods should be utilized to invite persons inside the church to enroll in Sunday School.

1. *Enroll those who attend Sunday School.*—There is an unwritten rule in many churches that a person must attend Sunday School three weeks in a row before he can be enrolled. If ministering is the priority, then it becomes legitimate to enroll persons the first time they attend, if they agree to be enrolled. Every person who attends Sunday School should be invited to enroll in Sunday School. Some may decline because they are enrolled in Bible study elsewhere or live too far away to attend on a regular basis. But they should be the ones to label themselves visitors. The invitation to enroll should be extended. Many persons who attend Sunday School do not enroll because no one asked them to enroll. Sunday School leaders and members must be trained and encouraged to invite those who attend to join.

2. *Enroll persons in the worship service.*—Inviting persons to enroll in Sunday School should be a regular part of the worship service. One way to accomplish this is to print a Sunday School enrollment form on the back of the church visitor's card. When guests are recognized in the worship service, invite them to enroll in Sunday School. During the following week, persons who enrolled should be contacted by someone in the appropriate class, given literature, and told where the class meets.

In one Sunday morning worship service where the attendance was much larger than the number that had been in Sunday School, we distributed enrollment cards to every person. Those who were already Sunday School members were asked to re-enroll. Those who were not members were invited to join. A total of ninety-three new persons were enrolled in Sunday School that day. A side benefit was that the cards of the Sunday School members included many new addresses and telephone numbers so that records could be updated.

3. *Enroll people when they join the church.*—When people join the church, the card they fill out should include the line, "Enroll me in Sunday School. Already ____, Yes ____, No ____." If the person agrees to be enrolled, follow-up by someone from the Sunday School class is immediate. Efforts are made to involve the person in regular Bible study and in other activities of the church. I am convinced that one of the reasons most churches have many members they can't locate is that the members were not cultivated. They never got acquainted with other church members. They did not become a part of a small group where they experienced love

and concern. They did not encounter the Word of God in a regular, systematic way.

These three methods for enrolling people in Sunday School all take place inside the church. Enrolling people in Sunday School should also take place outside the church, anywhere and anytime a person agrees to be enrolled. The concept is called open enrollment.

4. *Open Enrollment*—Sunday School leaders and members must be trained and equipped to enroll people in Bible study. Many of the same methods for discovering prospects can be used in enrolling persons. For example, when a survey is conducted, those not enrolled in any systematic Bible study should be first invited to enroll in Sunday School. Those who don't agree to be enrolled become prospects for further cultivation. In addition to all methods of face-to-face contact, persons may be invited by telephone to enroll in Sunday School. Letters with return cards may also be used. Letters should be prepared for church members not enrolled in Sunday School, parents of children not enrolled, visitors to Sunday School and worship services, and prospects. The letters should be signed by the pastor and include postage-paid cards whereby people may enroll in Sunday School by mail.

To enroll people, Sunday School leaders and members must have enrollment cards they can carry with them at all times. Small enrollment cards the size of a business card may be printed or purchased. Also, they may carry a supply of cards with the name and address of the church and the times of Sunday School and worship services. When someone agrees to be enrolled in Sunday School, he should be given the church card.

Sunday School leaders and members need to be asked to commit themselves to making regular efforts to enroll persons in Sunday School. In fact, commitment cards should be distributed at the beginning of the church year or perhaps every three months asking persons to commit themselves to enrolling one person each quarter, month, or week.

Those who enroll persons in Bible study should be affirmed and recognized for their efforts. A letter from the pastor is one method. Another is to list in the church newsletter the names of new members and those who enrolled them. Leaders in one church made a "Wall of Fame" board where the names of new members and those who enrolled them were posted.

Two central files need to be maintained to keep accurate enroll-ment records. The first is a master Sunday School membership file. The operating policy for the Sunday School should be that names are added and dropped only through the church office. Slips should be filled out on Sundays in the classes and depart-ments and then changes made in the central file and the class and department books during the week. This is the only way accurate records can be maintained. The second central file is the drop slip file. When a person is dropped, the reason is stated on the request slip—died, moved away, joined another church, etc. Occasionally, mistakes are made in the dropping of names. If the drop slips are kept, the records information is maintained and the person could easily be put back in the membership file if needed.

As prospects are discovered, regular efforts must be made to enroll them in Sunday School so that they can become a part of a class where love is expressed, needs are met, the Bible is taught, and the gospel is encountered.

REACHING THOSE WHO ARE HARD TO REACH

Some persons are very difficult to involve in a Sunday School class. They may be afraid of being asked to pray aloud or answer a question. Others find it easy to say no to invitations to participate in Bible study. Whatever the reason, there are persons in every community who will never be reached for Christ through efforts to involve them in a regular, ongoing Sunday School class.

The pastor's class is a tool for reaching these persons, involving them in Bible study, and eventually transferring most to regular Sunday School classes.

Before beginning the class, a pastor must specify two ground rules. First, the pastor will only attempt to enroll in his class those who have not agreed to be enrolled in other classes or persons the church has made no effort to reach. Second, no one already en-rolled in Sunday School may enroll in the pastor's class. The pur-pose of the class is to reach persons who would not otherwise agree to be enrolled in Bible study. The pastor's class is an up-graded adult class taught by the pastor during the Sunday School hour. The pastor's job is to feed the sheep. However, if he can't get the sheep to the food, he can't feed them. The pastor's class is simply a tool for getting the sheep to the food.

A meeting place must be selected that is easily accessible. Those who attend will not be familiar with the layout of the church. The auditorium is not the best place to start the class; but if that is the only space available, it can be used.

The initial job of enrolling people in the class belongs to the pastor. When I was a pastor, I began with the church members not enrolled in Sunday School and spent time on the telephone each day calling them to invite them to enroll in the class. By the time I finished, I had enrolled 93 percent of them in Sunday School—not all in the pastor's class. A couple who had just joined the church were willing to join an age-graded class. I also discovered the needs for ministries the church didn't offer, such as Sunday School provisions for the homebound. Preschoolers, children, and youth of adults who enrolled in the pastor's class were enrolled in ongoing classes and departments.

After the pastor has concentrated on church members not enrolled in Sunday School, he should begin contacting the general public. I took the telephone directory, began with "A," and went through the book. My basic approach was: "Hello, Bill. I am Andy Anderson, pastor of Riverside Baptist Church here in Fort Myers. You probably do not know me, but I know you because (reasons varied—doctor, politician, teacher, business, newspaper article, etc.). Bill, I am teaching a nondenominational Bible class each Sunday morning at 9:45 in the auditorium of our church. I want you and your family in my class if you are not enrolled in some other Bible study class."

Often the conversation continued something like this: "Andy, I really appreciate your invitation, but we are Methodists (Catholic, Presbyterian, etc.)."

"That's good, but are you involved in a systematic Bible study?" I then asked.

"Well, no, we're not," was often the reply. "Actually, when we go to church it is usually to the worship service."

I would then continue: "May I suggest something? Would you permit me to enroll you in my Bible class? You can study with us at 9:45 and then go on to your church for the worship service. I make you this promise—I will not ask you to become a Baptist."

At one time I had fourteen different denominations represented in my pastor's class. Our task is not to make Baptists. It is to teach the Scriptures. When this is done, the Holy Spirit convicts, converts, and places in our churches those whom He chooses to place there.

At least four groups of people generally will be attracted to the pastor's class: first, persons with emotional or educational problems that limit their ability to participate in a small group. They want and need Bible study but fear being singled out in a small group.

A second group is composed of highly intelligent persons who have the idea that Bible study can't be helpful unless it is taught by someone with a seminary degree. When I invited an attorney to join my pastor's class, his response was, "I would love to study with a professional." While it is certainly true that many of the finest Bible teachers do not have a great deal of formal education, many unsaved, well-educated persons do not understand this. These are more likely to respond to an invitation from the pastor to study with him.

A third group consists of people who have refused to enroll in Sunday School because they don't believe it will enhance their social standing. However, they also are more likely to say yes to an invitation from the pastor to be in his class. While this is certainly not the best motive for enrolling in Bible study, we must accept people as they are and then try to lead them to where they should be. The newly elected sheriff of the county was one of the persons who agreed to be enrolled in my pastor's class. Within a few weeks he, his wife, and several other members of his family had come into our church. He then asked for enrollment cards and, within a few days, enrolled forty-three persons—deputy sheriffs and their spouses and children.

Fourth, wealthy persons are often more likely to enroll initially in a class taught by the pastor.

One pastor set a personal goal to enroll five people a week in his class. At the end of the first three months he had enrolled sixty-one people. He fell short of his goal by four. However, this was the largest net increase in Sunday School enrollment the church had experienced in twelve years and was accomplished in three months.

At the beginning of the fourth month the pastor selected twenty men who were in the same age bracket, invited them to his home for a hamburger fry, showed them why they needed to be in a smaller class, presented their new teacher, distributed curriculum material, and started a new men's class with seventeen enrolled. Three of the men did not choose to transfer, so they remained in the pastor's class which now had forty-four enrolled.

During the following month, the pastor continued to enroll five per week, increasing his class size to sixty-four. At this time he selected twenty-five women who were in the same age group, invited them to his home, showed them why they needed to be in a smaller class, introduced their new teacher, distributed the literature, and started a new adult class with twenty-four enrolled. One returned to the pastor's class. The new enrollment in the pastor's class was forty. He continued to enroll five new people a week and during the next month exceeded his goal of twenty by enrolling twenty-six. The enrollment in the pastor's class increased to sixty-six. The pastor had received several requests for a coeducational class. He used the same method and started a class with thirty-one.

After six months, this pastor is continuing to enroll one person a day, five days a week. The net results of six months were: gross enrollment gain, 121; net enrollment gain, 113; three new adult classes (combined enrollment), 76; pastor's class enrollment, 37. His plans are to continue his present enrollment goal of five per week and the establishment of one new adult class each month. Because the new classes are made up of people of the same age group, these are placed in the proper department of the Sunday School; therefore, the grading system is not disturbed.

To operate the pastor's class several officers are needed. First is a class president. His/her job is to convene the class each Sunday and to oversee the organization. Second is the outreach leader who is responsible for enlisting one group leader for each six members and seeing that they contact each member every week. Third is a secretary to maintain the records. Fourth is a welcome committee to meet people, distribute name tags, help people get acquainted with each other, and serve coffee, orange juice, and doughnuts as people gather each week. Many people in the pastor's class will have never attended church or won't have attended for many years. They need assistance in meeting people and feeling comfortable.

The fellowship time should last thirty minutes. Then the president convenes the class with a very brief opening statement and turns the class over to the pastor, who teaches in a lecture format for thirty minutes. It is important that the pastor teach and resist the temptation to preach. He should read the Scripture and talk to the members about the passage. It is important to have material that members can study during the week. I recommend the Bible Book Series for Adults published by the Southern Baptist Sunday School Board.

After the class has been in operation three months, the pastor should select fifteen to twenty members who are near the same age and invite them to his home for dinner or dessert. At his home, he tells them, for the sake of their spiritual growth, they need to be in a smaller class where they can raise questions and share concerns. He introduces them to someone from the pastor's class who will be the teacher of this new class and asks them to be a part of it. My experience has been that most, sometimes all, will agree. Those who don't agree should continue in the pastor's class. In this way, the pastor's class becomes a "feeder class" to the ongoing Sunday School. With the new class reducing the membership of the pastor's class, the pastor continues enrolling new people. Within a month or whenever the class has grown to the size at which another new class can be started, the pastor repeats the process.

In one year, if the pastor enrolls one adult a day five days a week, he will enroll approximately 250 people. Because all of the members will be contacted each week, the average attendance in the Sunday School will increase approximately 125 just from those enrolled initially in the pastor's class. As many as 10 new adult classes will be started, and between 30 and 50 adults will be baptized the first year. Of course, the preschoolers, children, and youth of adults in the pastor's class will be participating in ongoing classes with their age group, further increasing the attendance.

Once the pastor's class gets started, the people in the class begin to invite business associates, friends, and family; and the growth accelerates.

Another pastor used this method to enroll 2,000 people in two years. He uses newspaper advertising and makes 100-150 telephone calls each week. He calls the pastor's class "a bridge between our city and the church."

ALTERNATIVES TO CLEANING THE ROLLS

This chapter has outlined ways to increase participation by reaching people not presently enrolled in any Bible study. Another group that needs attention is persons who are enrolled but do not attend. In many churches, names of persons who don't attend are periodically removed from the Sunday School rolls. When this happens, these persons are also removed from any opportunity for personal contact or ministry or to hear and accept the gospel.

People who have agreed to be enrolled in Sunday School and have attended usually quit attending for one of two reasons: (1) they fell out of fellowship with the Sunday School teacher or a member; (2) they feel nobody cares about them. Instead of giving up on these and dropping them from the Sunday School rolls, consider the following alternatives as ways of reaching and reclaiming persons.

1. *Transfer them to the pastor's class.*—Personal contact and attention from the pastor may be what many persons need to begin attending again. If this is the case, when the person is reclaimed for weekly Bible study, efforts should be undertaken as soon as it is appropriate to transfer the person to a class.

2. *Contact absentees.*—Begin through ongoing classes a regular, concerted effort to contact absentees. For at least three months, make sure that every absentee is contacted each week by personal visits, telephone calls, and letters. Assurance that they are missed and cared about will cause some persons to begin attending again. Also, through these contacts needs will be discovered that will become opportunities for ministry.

3. *Start a new class.*—This method is especially helpful with persons who quit attending because of a relationship problem with the teacher or a class member. When they are presented with an opportunity to join another class, many will attend.

4. *Start a special needs class.*—Some persons may not attend because they or a family member have a special need that cannot be met through existing classes. Special needs classes may include those for mentally retarded persons or deaf persons. Crisis needs may require classes which persons can attend temporarily to get help in dealing with the crisis. These may include working through divorce or dealing with grief. A class for newlyweds may need to be organized. When people see that their need can be met, they will attend.

5. *Start a weektime class.*—Some people may quit attending because their job requires them to work on Sundays. They still need Bible study and may respond to an invitation to join a class meeting during the week. In the United States today, approximately 40 percent of the adult population cannot attend church on Sunday. These persons are automatically excluded if we only offer Bible study on Sundays.

6. *Start a new Sunday School.*—There may be persons who don't attend because of language, economic, or cultural barriers. Perhaps a new Sunday School for a language group or a Sunday School meeting in a housing project or in a community separated from the church by a bridge or interstate could be a way to both reclaim nonattenders and reach new people.

7. *Begin an intercessory prayer ministry.*—Make a list of chronic absentees and enlist the help of persons to pray daily for these people and to pray that active Sunday School members will be willing to minister to them. In this way barriers of broken relationships and other problems that could not be solved in human terms may be broken down through God's power.

50 WAYS to find New People for Sunday School

1. List unchurched families from Vacation Bible School records.
2. Conduct an inside census.
3. Locate newcomers by calling all new listings in phone directory.
4. Update a former community survey.
5. Ask youth to survey blocks in which they live.
6. Compare church recreation participants to Sunday School rolls.
7. Subscribe to newcomer service for information.
8. Locate homebound by publishing lists and asking for update.
9. Use telephone directory to survey an entire telephone exchange.
10. Subscribe to *Legal News* for information on new homeowners.
11. Canvass university dormitories for unchurched.
12. Check college admissions office for church preferences of students.
13. Request information from managers of mobile home parks.
14. Call college placement offices for newly employed.
15. Identify shift workers through church survey.
16. Gather information on those who work in hospitals.
17. Survey membership for those who are food service workers.
18. Survey membership for those who are hotel and motel employees.
19. List church members who work on Sundays.
20. Contact international clubs for information on foreign students.
21. Confer with military base chaplains for unchurched families.
22. Use the door-to-door survey to locate unchurched people.
23. Request business people to identify associates who are un-churched.
24. Request church members to identify neighbors who are un-churched.
25. Identify unenrolled parents of children enrolled in Sunday School.
26. Identify unchurched parents of children enrolled in church day schools, kindergartens, and day-care centers.
27. Request mail response from radio audience.
28. Secure names from Dial-a-Devotional service.
29. Survey by phone newcomers listed by utilities turn-ons.
30. Use "I Know a Prospect" cards throughout the church.
31. Follow up on information received from Sunday School visitors.
32. Follow up on information received from church worship visitors.
33. Request information on newcomers from real estate agents.
34. Secure information on the families of mentally retarded.
35. Check church roll against Sunday School roll for Bible study prospects.
36. Identify unchurched persons in one's vocation, discipline, and/or professional club.
37. Locate persons in correctional institutions desiring Bible study.
38. Glean local newspaper for information on newlyweds.
39. Check the hospital reports in newspapers for names of new babies.
40. Enclose a "return card" in graduates' congratulations.
41. Send congratulations to those who have been reported achieving any public recognition.

42. Check all family members of babies enrolled in Cradle Roll department.
43. Use cross-reference directories to survey apartment houses.
44. Provide Outreach-Ministry forms for ongoing prospect reporting.
45. Provide guest book in church lobby to identify visitors to weddings, funerals, and other meetings at the church.
46. Register attendance of every person who attends revival.
47. Provide social events for parents without partners.
48. Secure information from administrators of senior adult centers.
49. Conduct an age-group hunt of a specific area and age.
50. Use special registration forms for church events such as concerts, dramas, etc.

6

Quality Product

Quality Bible teaching happens in churches in which the overarching commitment is to guide people into a study of the Bible as God's Holy Word to enable them to have a life-changing encounter with Jesus Christ as their Savior or to grow in their faith in Christ. Quality is evident as persons get to know each other, share their concerns, and ask questions. Quality is practiced as new persons are reached and quantitative growth is experienced. When people's needs are met through the ministry of a Sunday School class, quality is evident.

How is quality in teaching, reaching, and ministering developed and maintained? Attention must be given to nine key areas: (1) organization; (2) workers; (3) training; (4) planning; (5) space; (6) worship services; (7) money; (8) image; (9) communications.

ORGANIZATION

The Sunday School is not organized only on the basis of how teaching will take place on Sunday mornings. The Sunday School must also be organized for reaching and ministry. Most Sunday Schools are organized to take care of the people who are enrolled. In a Sunday School where growth is a priority, the organization needs to be developed to accommodate the prospects, those who need to be reached.

As a general rule of thumb, I believe a Sunday School needs to have one teaching unit for each 15-18 enrollees in order to be in a growth posture rather than a maintenance position. The ratio for each age group will differ. For example, the enrollment ceiling in a department for babies should be 12; ages 2-3, 20; and ages 4-5, 25. For children in grades one through six, no department should have more than 30. In a department for junior high youth the ceiling should be 50 with classes no larger than 10; for senior high youth a department ceiling of 60 and a class limit of 15. With adults, no department should be larger than 125 or classes larger than 25.

When these organizational guidelines are followed, two positive factors take place. First, the Sunday School is in a position to grow because rooms are not filled to capacity and workers do not have more than they can do. Second, units are small enough that individual ministry can take place. Remember, the Sunday School is a ministry organization.

For example, consider a widowed mother who has a fifteen-year-old son. Both are active in the church. But one Saturday night the mother receives a telephone call that her son has been arrested for selling marijuana. She is crushed. What does she do? Who does she call for help and support? If she is a member of a Sunday School class of thirty-five to fifty women who generally listen while the teacher lectures, the mother may not view the class or its members as a resource in a time of trouble.

However, if she is in a class of twenty-five where twelve to fifteen attend each week and habitually share their concerns and pray for each other, chances are greater that this woman will call the teacher or a class member. The class will then be able to surround the mother with love, concern, and help.

It is imperative that personalized ministry take place within Sunday School teaching units. This requires units that are small enough to facilitate active, caring concern. It is at this point that leaders of the Sunday School should study the records to determine how many classes and departments are presently organized, the enrollment of each, and whether and where additional units are needed.

As this task is undertaken, leaders need to be aware of three barriers to effective Sunday School organization. First is overly strong attachment by members to one teacher. One of the best signs of a good teacher is one who develops people who can move out of the class into leadership positions. A good teacher is not necessarily one who can draw great numbers to him/herself. The second barrier to effective Sunday School organization is members who are overly attached to their class and refuse to transfer. The third barrier is overly strong attachment to a meeting room.

The overall solution to all three barriers is annual reorganization of the Sunday School. A growing Sunday School will have to be reorganized each year to add new units and redistribute enrollment to have the proper unit size. In the process, people are less likely to develop overly strong attachments to their teacher, class, or room.

While a major reorganization of the Sunday School should take place once a year, new classes may be started any time as needs are discovered.

One method for discovering where new adult classes are needed is through the use of an Adult Profile Chart (see example). When completed, the chart helps adult class members and leaders see adult classes in clear perspective: (1) how classes are graded; (2) how classes overlap; (3) where gaps exist in reaching people.

To make and use an Adult Profile Chart, secure the correct ages of all enrolled adults. Prepare a wall chart showing a line for each beginning with age eighteen and divided for men and women. Beginning with the youngest class place a hash-mark for each adult on the line of his or her proper age. If classes are made up of both men and women, place hash-marks near center line. When all class members are indicated, draw a balloon around the marks for the class. Do this for each adult class. Study chart for gaps and overlaps.

Prospects may be indicated with additional hash-marks; but re-group classes by enrollment, not prospects. The number of prospects available may influence the projected size of additional classes or teaching units. Indicate possible regrouping by horizontal lines across the chart.

A second tool for starting new classes is a Class Creation Worksheet. In the left-hand column place the name of each Sunday School class or department. In the second column, place the name of each teacher. The age range of each unit should be listed in the third column. The fourth column should be titled "New Classes" and used when a new unit needs to be created from an existing one. List the names of the two classes, their teachers, and the age ranges and meeting places for each. By this means the Sunday School organization can be enlarged to minister to the needs of the people who are presently enrolled. Exercise care in creating new units to be sure they are large enough to gain momentum and grow. Units that are too small may lose momentum and die.

Following are some possible new units that may need to be started (see New Start Decision Sheet). When one unit has too wide an age span or one class has become too large, a new one may need to be started. Classes for single adults or senior adults may need to be considered. Consider a special class for church members not enrolled in Sunday School or internationals. Special classes to minister to adults away (college students, military, workers temporarily transferred) or homebound persons may be needed. In addition to weektime ministries for the homebound, a Sunday morning class by telephone hookup may be an option. Sunday School classes in nursing homes, jails, prisons, or other institutions may provide a much-needed ministry. Classes for the mentally retarded or deaf should be offered if the need exists.

Where a lack of space is the major limiting factor in a church's ability to grow, a second Sunday School may be needed. Where a high percentage of people work on Sunday, providing a Sunday School on another day may be a solution.

The key to looking at the Sunday School organization and enlarging the organization to meet needs is learning to think outside traditional lines of how things are done in churches. When a church knows who the people are who need to be reached and what their needs are, then it must extend and expand the organization to meet the needs.

WORKERS

Let's return to the premise stated earlier that the Sunday School is a ministering organization. Teaching units must be organized on a small enough basis that ministry can happen. Similarly, ministry will not take place without sufficient workers. A Sunday School needs a ratio of at least one worker for each eight members to facilitate effective ministry, outreach, and teaching. If the ratio is greater than one to eight, this will not happen and the average attendance will be approximately one-third of the membership.

Several years ago I conducted 38 comparative studies of churches which illustrate the importance of having at least one worker for every 8 members.

For example, I studied one Sunday School with 190 enrolled and one with 188 enrolled. The Sunday School with 190 members had a worker ratio of 1 to 19, an average of eight outreachers per week making 20 contacts and an average attendance of 60 (32 percent of enrollment).

On the other hand, the church with 188 members had a worker ratio of 1 to 5, an average of 18 visitors making 133 weekly contacts and an average attendance of 120 (64 percent of the enrollment).

Regardless of the size of the Sunday School, a much higher attendance was the result when the Sunday School had a worker ratio of no more than 1 to 8. When the worker ratio is more than 1 to 8, only the hardcore of the faithful who are going to come whether or not ministry is taking place (about one-third of the membership) will attend. Very little ministry or discipleship is taking place. New church members are not being enrolled in Sunday School, nurtured in their faith, ministered to, and helped to grow. The tragedy of this is that a church does not have the right to birth babies (lead people to Christ) and leave them outdoors (fail to lead them to grow).

In conclusion, in a Sunday School where the ratio of workers to enrollment remains the same, the percentage of attendance to enrollment will remain unchanged. When the ratio of workers to enrollment decreases, yet remains above 1 to 8, the percentage of attendance will not increase. However, when the ratio of workers to enrollment decreases, and drops to at least 1 to 8, the percentage of attendance of enrollment increases. For each point the ratio of workers to enrollment increases, the percentage of attendance to enrollment decreases 2 to 3 percent.

TRAINING

In a church where the Sunday School enrollment is increasing and efforts are being made to enlarge the organization and provide more workers, a continual worker training process is needed. Following is a suggested training process which should be repeated every three months to provide enough trained workers for a growing Sunday School.

1. Determine the number of needed workers.

2. Select the teacher or teachers for the training course.

3. Enlist the support of Sunday School leaders and members in praying for new workers. When the praying has begun, the process of enlisting new workers should be started.

4. Enlist the workers. This job does not have to be difficult if people are praying that God will call out the needed workers. He will honor these prayers. Allow five weeks for enlistment.

5. Begin the class. The teacher should start the class on the sixth Sunday of each quarter to continue for eight weeks. The class should meet three times each week—Sunday morning, Sunday night, and one night during the week.

6. Teach the class. Class sessions should include an overview of the purpose of the Sunday School, outreach, weekly workers' meetings. Members should visit and observe in classes and departments of each age group and discuss their observations. Teaching should also emphasize the importance of teaching the Bible and how this is accomplished with each age group.

7. Class graduation. When the class completes its work after eight weeks, each person will have had twenty-four hours of training before they began their task as workers.

When this process is followed, my studies have shown that 93 percent of those who start the class complete it and accept some responsibility in the Sunday School. In addition, some present workers will request to take a leave of absence to take the training. People want to be more effective workers and will take the training when they see a way to do so.

Even as this training for potential workers is offered quarterly, additional short-term, specialized training for workers with each age group needs to be offered. Also, task-related training needs to be provided for administrators, teachers, and outreachers.

PLANNING

The most important meeting that takes place in a church is the Sunday School weekly workers' meeting. Planning is essential for effective teaching, outreach, and ministry.

There are four essentials for an effective weekly workers' meeting. The first is *leadership support*. The pastor must be in favor of it and involved in it. Second is *priority in time scheduling*. Nothing must be allowed to interfere or conflict with weekly workers' meeting. Third, Sunday School workers must be *expected to attend*. Fourth, the meeting must *support and enhance* what happens on Sunday morning. The weekly workers' meeting generates successful Sunday School work.

Weekly workers' meeting format—The weekly workers' meeting should last at least one hour. It should begin with a ten-minute general session for all workers. The pastor should use five minutes to motivate the workers. The other five minutes will be used for general announcements. After ten minutes workers divide by age groups or Sunday School departments. The first part of the time should be used for reviewing and evaluating the previous Sunday, planning upcoming events, coordinating assignments, sharing concerns and needs, and praying for these. For the last twenty to thirty minutes, the director and teachers should plan the Sunday session while the outreach people plan visitation and make assignments for contacts.

SPACE

One of the greatest barriers to growth in many places is a lack of space. A lack of vision in building too small and the inability to acquire additional land are two major reasons many churches have stopped growing. However, I believe that because God is more interested in our reaching people than we are, He will enable us to have the space we need and to pay for the space. There are six major ways to acquire additional space.

#1—Utilize available space. Engage an outside person to do a space walk of the church facilities. Walk through every available room. One of the discoveries often made is that rooms that could house Sunday School classes and departments are often being used to store materials which may never be used again. Hay bales from last year's nativity scene, angel wings, broken furniture, old literature, and many other items may need to be cleaned out of the building and thrown away. The space being occupied by these

items should be used to enable boys and girls, men and women to study the Bible. Church buildings are not for junk storage. As a general rule, approximately 15 percent additional space can be gained just by cleaning house and throwing away junk.

A second discovery from a space walk may be that rooms intended primarily for other purposes could double as Sunday School space. For example, a class could meet in the kitchen. A fellowship hall or recreation area could be partitioned with room dividers to house several classes. It is important to note that three to five classes may meet satisfactorily in a large room, whereas two classes may have difficulty. With several classes, the sound of voices blurs and is not distracting. But with two classes, the voices may compete with one another and be disruptive. A stage may become a Sunday School classroom. Several classes can be housed in the worship center or auditorium—one in each corner, one in the choir loft, and one in the balcony.

#2—Adjust the available space. Study the size of the groups meeting in each room and make adjustments as needed. For example, a large class may be cramped in a small room and a small class wasting space in a larger room. These two groups may exchange places, and both may have room to grow. Departments for preschoolers and children need more square feet per person than classes for youth and adults.

#3—Adapt available space. Shortly after I began working as a growth specialist for the Baptist Sunday School Board, I visited a church which had no educational space and, therefore, no Sunday School. Because of this the church had not grown for twenty years. A new pastor was called to the church. He led the people to remove the pews from the worship center. They purchased chairs and constructed L-shaped dividers. By this method, they acquired eleven classrooms for Bible study in space that could also be used for worship when the dividers were pushed against the outside walls. Then teachers and workers for the Sunday School were enlisted and trained. A survey of the community was conducted. Prospects were discovered and a visitation program begun. When the Sunday School was started, twice as many persons attended as had ever come to a worship service at the church. Today the church has both a worship center and an educational building. But they began their growth by adapting their existing space.

#4—Start a second Sunday School. If a church is not able to build or locate additional space, two or more Sunday Schools can be organized to meet at different times on Sunday morning and utilize the same space. For some churches this is a temporary solution; others plan to maintain multiple Sunday Schools on a permanent basis. A church should not attempt to change to multiple worship or Sunday Schools unless or until a need exists. When church members see the need, they are more likely to participate in making it a success.

Following are actions to consider when planning multiple Sunday Schools:

1. Seek the leadership of the Holy Spirit in making decisions.
2. Contact other churches who are already conducting multiple Sunday Schools.
3. Begin several months in advance to discuss this option with the church leaders.
4. Follow church policy in presenting the plan to the church.
5. Use committees to develop suggested solutions to the problems related to preschool needs, traffic flow both inside and outside of the building, the use of facilities and rooms, schedule, and leadership.
6. Survey church members to determine which Sunday School they desire to attend. Special efforts may need to be made to urge enough families to enroll in the new school to ensure its success.
7. On the basis of expected attendance and enrollment, determine the organizational structure needed for each school. Enlist the leadership and assign the rooms and facilities.
8. Enroll members in the proper Sunday School and prepare separate and complete records for each school.
9. Be sure that inactive Sunday School members are enrolled in one of the schools.
10. Set the date for the plan to begin. Publicize the beginning date and send information to every home explaining rooms, teachers, age divisions, schedule, and other items of interest.

#5—Secure adjacent space. After a space walk of the church facilities is completed, continue the walk through the community. Walk about one-half mile in each direction from the church. What buildings might be available to rent or use? A school? Lodge hall? Bank?

Vacant buildings? House? Shopping mall? Funeral home? Homes of church members? Hotel or motel? Space is usually available if we open our eyes to the possibilities.

#6—Secure additional space. A general rule of thumb in buying property is that two acres are needed for each three hundred persons in attendance. This assumes level property with moderate setback requirements. This space will allow for parking, landscaping, a small playground, and adequate light and ventilation. A general guideline for educational space is forty-five square feet per person. Buildings should be planned in light of present enrollment and planned growth. It is tragic and an illustration of shortsighted vision when a building is completed and the church has already outgrown it.

IMAGE

We live in an image-conscious society where appearance is important. While the appearance of the church building, grounds, and printed materials is not the most important thing about the church, appearance is a critical factor in first impressions. Based on a first impression, a person may feel drawn toward or away from involvement with the church.

A growing church should be an attractive church. Buildings should be clean, neat, and painted. Yards should be clean, landscaped, and trimmed. I visited a church that had a new million-dollar auditorium. The educational space was in the original building next door which had an old tin roof that had rusted. The members were not conscious of the appearance of the rusty roof. But when I approached the building for the first time, I saw the old roof before I saw the new modern auditorium.

Related to this, evaluate the quality of the printing of materials such as bulletins, newsletters, and other mailouts. Many churches use old equipment that results in a messy, shoddy appearance. Churches have the most important news to share, but we share it in a way that it appears smudged, messy, or hard to read. A church newsletter or mailout may be the basis on which an unreached person forms an image of the church.

COMMUNICATIONS

A growing church needs to emphasize communications, both internal and external.

Internally, it is vital that church members know what is happening before it happens. Growth by its very nature brings change. Change is difficult to cope with. Understanding what is taking place and why is an absolute necessity for members to be in a position to be cooperative. Communication needs to take place from the pulpit and in Sunday School classes and departments. Important information should be shared verbally and in writing through bulletins, newsletters, and correspondence. The importance of reaching people should be kept before the people through bulletin boards, displays, and all forms of written and spoken communication.

Externally, a growing church should advertise regularly. Newspaper ads should be run at least weekly. They should be large enough to be visible and placed on sports or entertainment pages rather than on the religion pages. Weekly "shopper" papers or suburban weeklies may be another advertising option at a lower rate than a metropolitan daily. Radio advertising may be another option. However, if the goal is to reach unchurched people, do not advertise on a Christian station. Television advertising may also be an option, even if only for a ten-second spot. Cable television advertising may be available at a low rate and still have a sizable audience.

Direct mail is another valuable tool. To be effective it must be used regularly, at least four times a year. While the cost may sound high at the time, if it is used to reach people, those who are brought in will increase the income of the church and direct mail will pay for itself.

A growing church must advertise, letting people know it exists to meet the needs of people.

WORSHIP

Several dimensions should be considered in the worship services of a growth-minded congregation.

First, change the order of service regularly. Don't do the same things the same way each week. An air of expectancy in which people don't know what is going to happen but feel that what does happen will be good and exciting is a vital part of meaningful worship. For example, in one service after a particularly inspirational music number, the pastor gave the invitation. It was the right moment. No sermon was needed.

Second, emphasize music. Music is about one-half the worship service. Music attracts people that preaching may not. Music speaks to people in ways that preaching cannot.

Third, preach the word. Many growing churches today are led by expository preachers who take a book of the Bible, read it, and then work with the people.

Fourth, learn how to give an invitation. Use the choir to make a smooth transition into the invitation. I believe the pastor should stay in the pulpit and let counselors receive those who come. Counselors should be trained soul-winners. Or if the pastor receives those who come forward, he should then bring in a counselor to follow up so he can receive others. When new members are introduced to the congregation, someone from their Sunday School class should be invited to stand with them. This begins the transition of helping the person get acquainted and become a part of a small group.

MONEY

God is under no obligation to support a Christian club. A Christian club is a church that is not growing. The obligation of a church is to carry out the Great Commission. If it fails at this task, it will not grow. Money problems follow. A nongrowing church increases its income only with inflation income as tithers receive salary increases and, in turn, increase their giving. Three signs point to money problems: (1) the church cuts back on the literature and other materials and supplies it purchases; (2) the church cuts back on gifts to missions; (3) staff salaries are not increased.

On the other hand, God has promised to supply all the needs of a New Testament church. God's plan of finance is not tithes and offerings. God's plan of finance is people. When church people are involved in reaching people, God gives the money to finance the church. This can occur in the following ways. First, determine the weekly financial needs of the church. Second, determine the present average per-capita weekly giving into the weekly financial need. The answer is the Sunday School attendance needed to bring in enough money to meet weekly obligations. When this figure is known, goals and strategies need to be developed to reach the people and involve them in Bible study. They will also give the money needed to support the church.

In conclusion, a quality church program for a growing church includes multifaceted dimensions—organization, workers, training, planning, space, image consciousness, effective communication, attention to worship services, and a people-based philosophy of money. All are important and must receive constant attention as new people are reached and as the congregation grows and changes.

NEW START DECISION SHEET
Classes/Departments/Sunday Schools

Directions: This sheet lists areas of need you may find. (1) Go through list; check each area that applies to your Sunday School. (2)Now check in the "will do" column each area in which you'll make a start; write in the date in the "now" or "later" column.

Start Need	Need to Start	I Will Do	Now (Date)	Later (Date)
1. An adult class from a "too wide a span class"				
2. An adult class from a "too large" class				
3. A class for single adults				
4. A class for younger single adults				
5. A class for older singles				
6. A class for formerly marrieds (single again)				
7. A class for internationals				
8. A class for senior adults not being reached				
9. A class for median adults not being reached				
10. A class for young adults not being reached				
11. A class for unenrolled church members				
12. A pastor's class				
13. A college students away department				
14. An adults away department				
15. A homebound department				
16. A class by telephone hookup for homebounds				
17. A class in a nursing home				
18. A class in a jail or prison				
19. A class for Sunday workers				
20. A class for mentally retarded				
21. A class for deaf				
22. A class for language group				
23. From one to two Youth departments				
24. A Youth department for each high school grade				
25. A Youth department for each junior high grade				
26. Two Youth classes for any grade with 11 enrolled				
27. From one to two Children's departments				
28. From two to three Children's departments				
29. From three to six Children's departments				
30. A class for mentally retarded children				

Quality Product

Start Need	Need to Start	I Will Do	Now (Date)	Later (Date)
31. A class for deaf children				
32. From one to two Preschool departments				
33. From two to three Preschool departments				
34. A separate department for fours and fives				
35. A Cradle Roll department				
36. A second Sunday School				
37. Start a new Sunday School				
38. Start a Friday night Sunday School				
39. Start a satellite Sunday School				
40. Other				

ADULT PROFILE CHART

This chart helps adult class members and leaders "see" adult classes in clear perspective revealing (1) how classes are graded; (2) how they overlap; and (3) where gaps in reaching people exist. The chart may be used further in planning new adult classes or Bible teaching units.

Here's how to make and use a chart.

1. Secure from Enrollment Cards the correct ages of all enrolled adults.

2. Prepare a wall chart showing a line for each beginning with age 18 and divided for men and women.

3. Beginning with the youngest class place a hash-mark for each adult on the line of his or her proper age. If classes are made up of both men and women, place hash-marks near center line.

4. When all class members are indicated draw a ballon around the marks for the class.

5. Do this for each adult class.

6. Study chart for gaps and overlaps.

7. Prospects may be indicated with additional hash-marks but regroup classes by enrollment, not prospects. The number of prospects available may influence the projected size of additional classes or teaching units.

8. Indicate possible regrouping by horizontal lines across the chart.

	MEN	WOMEN
18		1
19		1 111
20		1 11̶1̶1̶ Young
21		1 111 Married
22		1 11 18-2?
23	111	
24	11	11̶1̶1̶ 1
25	1	1 111
26		1 11̶1̶1̶ 11
27		11 Dorcas
28		1111 25—29
29	Men	11̶1̶1̶
30	25-33 1	1
31	11	111 11
32	111	
33	11̶1̶1̶	11 T.E.L.
34	1 111	111 30-35
35	11 11 11̶1̶1̶	11
36	1111	1
37	1	1 1
38		1
39	Men 11	1
40	34-45 11̶1̶1̶	11 Ready
41	111	11 30-43
42	1111	1
43	11 11̶1̶1̶	1
63		
64		
65		
66		
67		
68		

ORGANIZE THE SUNDAY SCHOOL FOR GROWTH

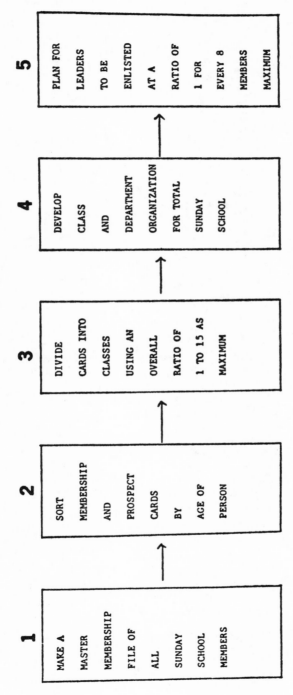

1
MAKE A
MASTER
MEMBERSHIP
FILE OF
ALL
SUNDAY
SCHOOL
MEMBERS

2
SORT
MEMBERSHIP
AND
PROSPECT
CARDS
BY
AGE OF
PERSON

3
DIVIDE
CARDS INTO
CLASSES
USING AN
OVERALL
RATIO OF
1 TO 15 AS
MAXIMUM

4
DEVELOP
CLASS
AND
DEPARTMENT
ORGANIZATION
FOR TOTAL
SUNDAY
SCHOOL

5
PLAN FOR
LEADERS
TO BE
ENLISTED
AT A
RATIO OF
1 FOR
EVERY 8
MEMBERS
MAXIMUM

SMALL CLASSES REACH MORE PERSONS FOR CHRIST THAN LARGE CLASSES

7

Caring Productivity

¹Now after this the Lord appointed seventy others, and sent them two and two ahead of Him to every city and place where He Himself was going to come.

²And He was saying to them, "The harvest is plentiful, but the laborers are few; therefore beseech the Lord of the harvest to send out laborers into His harvest.

³"Go your ways; behold, I send you out as lambs in the midst of wolves.

⁴"Carry no purse, no bag, no shoes; and greet no one on the way.

⁵"And whatever house you enter, first say, 'Peace be to this house.'

⁶"And if a man of peace is there, your peace will rest upon him; but if not, it will return to you.

⁷"And stay in that house, eating and drinking what they give you; for the laborer is worthy of his wages. Do not keep moving from house to house.

⁸"And whatever city you enter, and they receive you, eat what is set before you;

⁹and heal those in it who are sick, and say to them, 'The kingdom of God has come near to you.'

¹⁰"But whatever city you enter and they do not receive you, go out into its streets and say,

¹¹'Even the dust of your city which clings to our feet, we wipe off in protest against you; yet be sure of this, that the kingdom of God has come near.'

¹²"I say to you, it will be more tolerable in that day for Sodom, than for that city. . . .

¹⁶"The one who listens to you listens to Me, and the one who rejects you rejects Me; and he who rejects Me rejects the One who sent Me."

¹⁷And the seven returned with joy, saying, "Lord, even the demons are subject to us in Your name."

Luke 10:1-12,16-17 (NASB)

These verses from Luke 10 present God's plan of outreach which, if carried out, will result in the life needs of people being met, persons becoming involved in Bible study through a church, and many persons being won to Christ.

Seven key truths about outreach that results in caring productivity are highlighted in this passage.

First, we see in verse 1 that this is the Lord's plan, "The Lord appointed seventy others." This plan works because it is His.

Second, the plan includes all Christians. In chapter 9, Jesus first enlisted and sent out the twelve disciples. Then in chapter 10, he sent out the others also. God's plan is to involve all of his followers in carrying the gospel to the community and the ends of the earth.

Third, God's plan of outreach is a visitation plan. People are to leave the four walls of the church and go out into the community. It is not enough to have a beautiful building, an excellent program of ministry, and a good pastor. We are a sent people. We are a visiting people. At the same time, the people did not go out at random. The Lord organized them and sent them out two by two. God realizes the weakness of one person. A second is always present to strengthen, help, pray for, and encourage one who may be discouraged. God organized not only the people but also the geography. He sent them "to every city and place where He Himself was going to come." We must organize to avoid duplication of some visits while others would never see or hear.

In the fourth place, the Lord's plan of outreach is under his watchful eye. While there are occasions in all of our lives when we feel isolated from God, we can know we are under his watchful eye when we are visiting people on behalf of the Lord Jesus Christ.

Fifth, God's plan is thorough and specific. People were sent into every city and place. Christ died for all persons. Therefore, every city, every community, every street, every house, and every person must be contacted. Those who visited were to go back again and again to every home until every person had heard. Those who visited were to go representing Jesus. When we visit, we shouldn't go just to represent a church, a Sunday School class, or a pastor. We should go to represent Jesus.

Sixth, we see that God's outreach plan is imperative. Verse 2 states that the harvest is great. The harvest is made up of large numbers of people. Also, the harvest belongs to the Lord. Too often in our carelessness we fail to emphasize that the priority of the church is reaching people, gathering or reaping the harvest. The reason for the imperative dimension of being involved in outreach is that the laborers are few. There are many to be reached and few to reach them. Another reason that outreach is imperative is that those who go can know they go with God's authority. The Lord said, "When you go, you will be received by some. Enter those homes and let my peace go with you into the house. But when they do not receive you, it will be more tolerable in that day for Sodom than for that city" (author's paraphrase). This places an awesome responsibility on those who visit.

Finally, God's outreach plan is successful. Every plan the Lord gives us is successful when we carry it out as he designed it. In verse 17, we see that those who went out returned with joy. They said, "Lord, even the demons are subject to us in Your name."

HOW TO HAVE EFFECTIVE VISITATION

Sunday School is more than a Bible teaching organization. It is a ministering organization. The best way to minister to the needs of people is to meet them informally in their homes and businesses. This requires visitation. In observing the visitation program of thousands of churches, I've discovered a similarity in plans and methods of those experiencing the best results. What follows is a compilation of what I believe to be the best visitation plan. It may be implemented in different ways, but the various elements do need to be included.

In the first place, the pastor must lead the visitation program. If church members are going out, they want to know their pastor is not only supportive of their efforts but is leading them.

Second, during the Sunday School hour, people need to be pre-enlisted to participate in visitation during the week. One way to achieve this is to attach a 3" × 5" card to each class record book. (A printed Outreach Card is published by Broadman Supplies.) The card should include a space for the class name. Under that should be printed, "These will represent our class in visitation this week." Space should be left for names to be listed. Then the teacher or outreach leader should be responsible for seeing that at least two persons are enlisted from the class. Every Sunday School class should have at least one person visiting from it each week.

For Preschool and Children's departments, those who visit will be the adult workers. For Youth and Adult classes, both members and leaders will be encouraged to participate in visitation. For those who are willing to visit but cannot go out at the regular visitation time, assignments should be distributed on Sunday morning. Also, in Sunday School, announcements should be made encouraging participation in visitation.

Third, during the morning and evening services the pastor should make the announcements about visitation. This establishes the pastor as the leader of visitation and gives priority to it. The pastor's announcements should be specific concerning the need and his expectations. For example: "We have 25 teaching units in our Sunday School. I expect at least one person from each teaching unit to be present in visitation tomorrow night. I plan to be there." With this type of announcement the pastor emphasizes the importance of each class participating and places responsibility upon the classes to be involved. By reminding people that he personally leads the visitation program, he increases participation.

Fourth, visitation should be scheduled at a certain time each week. The best time is that in which the largest number of persons can participate. I have seen good visitation programs held on every day of the week. Even as church visitation is scheduled for one time, it should constantly be emphasized that people can and should visit at other times as well. The special time set aside for visitation becomes a stackpole.

Let us assume for the purpose of illustration that visitation is set for Monday night. Before people arrive, one table should be set up for each class or department. Three visitation books should be established for each class.

The first book is for *ministry visitation* and should include the names and addresses of each member of the class. Ministry visitation is contacting absentees or members with special needs such as those who are sick or who have recently experienced the death of a loved one.

The second book is for *enrollment visitation* and should include the names and addresses of persons who are prospects for Bible study. As mentioned in an earlier chapter, a class is in an ideal position to grow when it has a number of prospects equal to the enrollment.

The third book is for *evangelistic visitation* and includes the names and addresses of persons who are not Christians. This third book will be made up only for older Children, Youth, and Adult units.

There will be some duplication between the books. For example, some persons who do not know Christ will already be enrolled. Ministry may be involved in all three types of visitation. In ministry visitation the need may be known before the visit is made—illness, grief, etc. Whatever the primary purpose of the visit the persons who go should be sensitive to needs they may encounter and willing to become involved in meeting the needs.

These three books should be on the table designated for each unit. If a card-and-pocket system is used, the books should be open so that those going visiting can sign in and list the cards they are taking. A quick meal should be served on visitation night. Following the meal, the pastor should speak for three to five minutes. This should include words of motivation and a prayer of encouragement. In essence, he communicates to them through his words and actions: "Visitation is a priority of this church because Jesus commanded us to go. I believe visitation is important. I am going and I ask that you go also."

Then comes the time for visitation assignments. Some of those going out may desire to do ministry visitation—visiting class members. These may be persons who are extremely uncomfortable visiting people they don't know but want to be involved in ministering to members who have been absent or who are inactive. When these go out, they may learn that someone has quit attending due to serious illness or has a family member who is ill. Needs may be discovered that the entire class will become involved in meeting. Persons who go out to do ministry visitation may discover the person is angry about something that has happened at church or toward someone in the class. They may need to be involved in the ministry of listening or reconciliation.

Others who go out visiting may go primarily to attempt to enroll prospects in Sunday School. They will need to go with information about the church, Sunday School provisions for each age group, and a genuine interest in meeting people and inviting them to be involved in Bible study. Some of the persons they visit will have attended Sunday School, while others may be newcomers to the city or persons not presently involved in any formal Bible study.

Then there are the persons who prefer to do evangelistic visitation, winning people to Christ. They have been trained and are committed to sharing their own experience and attempting to win others to the Lord whenever possible. One thing I have observed is that, where there is an option, it is preferable to enroll lost people in Bible study *and then* lead them to the Lord. This is because they more easily see the value of Bible study and church involvement to their spiritual growth than when they are won to the Lord without having been involved in a church.

It is important that all three types of visitation take place simultaneously for two reasons. First, those who visit can choose the type they are most comfortable with. Second, when those who go out return for the report session, they will motivate one another. After the period of visitation, a brief time of reporting is imperative. Some will return discouraged because they found no one at home or had no positive results from their visits. These persons will need encouragement to return for visitation the next week. Others will have experienced high moments—enrolling someone in Bible study, leading someone to Christ, or meeting someone's need. These people need an opportunity to share their experience.

A variety of methods of reporting may be used—everyone returning to the church or persons gathering in small groups by neighborhoods, for example. The reporting session will provide the motivation by which participants see and hear firsthand the importance of going out each week.

A special visitation emphasis that should be conducted four times per year is Literature Distribution. This becomes an opportunity for Sunday School workers to personally visit members and prospects and give them their Bible study material before the start of the next quarter. The outreach leader is responsible for organizing and overseeing literature distribution to be sure that each member and prospect is provided a lesson periodical each quarter.

Literature distribution should take place the week before a new quarter begins. Those who go out should make the visit a fellowship and ministry opportunity rather than just giving the person the literature at the door. They should briefly overview the next quarter's Bible study theme while sharing the joy they experience in studying God's Word. They should share class and personal concerns and invite the person to share his own concerns. Teachers can gain valuable insights through these visits that will enable them to make Bible teaching/learning sessions more meaningful.

PERSONAL CONTACTS AND HIGH ATTENDANCE

As growth and enrolling people in Bible study are emphasized, it is also important to periodically emphasize attendance because many of the people being enrolled are not accustomed to attending Sunday School. I believe two things about high attendance days: (1) a church cannot be grown with high attendance days because normally attendance will increase on that day and then return to its original level the next week; (2) high attendance days should be held periodically because the excitement and extra effort generated by having them will result in some persons attending who otherwise would not have come.

A high attendance day should have a goal. The goal should be challenging but one that can be reached. One way to set a goal is to find out the highest attendance of each class in the last twelve months, total the figures, and add one. The total will be higher than the average attendance but will be attainable because every unit will have achieved its goal at least once. Adding one more represents a little extra challenge. Setting an unreachable goal will destroy the morale of the people. The purpose of high attendance days should be motivation to do the extra work involved in reaching people.

There are two ways to work with a goal for high attendance day. The first is to set the goal and announce it. It is talked about from the pulpit and in Sunday School. Announced goals are frequently not reached. The second method is the underwritten goal—that is, the attendance goal is underwritten by setting a second goal for contacts.

As with goals, there are two kinds of contacts. The first is an atmosphere-creating contact such as a general announcement. It creates an atmosphere that visitors are welcome and members are encouraged to attend regularly, but it doesn't result in much, if any, increased attendance.

The second type of contact is the quality contact—a personal telephone call, card, letter, or visit. These are the contacts that produce attendance.

An average of seven to ten quality contacts is needed to increase attendance by one when the contacts are made the week before the high attendance day. For example, if a church has an average Sunday School attendance of 200 and an average of 100 weekly contacts are made, then 107 to 110 contacts will be needed to attain an attendance of 201. Suppose a church has an average attendance of 400 in Sunday School and a high attendance day goal of 500. Normally, the church averages 100 weekly contacts. To reach the goal of 500, a total of 1,100 contacts will be needed—100 to sustain the average attendance of 400 and 1,000 (10 times 100) to achieve the goal of 500.

People will not make 1,100 contacts in one week just because someone stands up on Sunday morning and says that is what is needed. But if they are given a method for making the contacts and the contact goal is emphasized, people are more likely to respond. Then if the contact goal is achieved, the attendance goal will also be reached. The problem in many churches over the years has been that high attendance goals have been set but without supporting plans, strategies, and goals for contacts. Therefore, the high attendance goals too often are never reached.

There are many methods for reaching contact goals. One is a

telephone contact system in which the pastor calls the minister of education. He calls age-group division directors who call department directors. Department directors call teachers who call outreach leaders. Outreach leaders call group leaders who call members and prospects. In a very short period of time, all members and prospects can be personally contacted about being present in Sunday School the next Sunday. Two other methods are campaigns, "I'll Be One of the Bunch" or "Don't Break the Chain." These are methods whereby people are contacted and asked to agree to be present the next Sunday.

In setting goals, remember that no goal can be attained until it is broken down to the lowest common denominator—a class goal for a high attendance day or a weekly goal for a year's net gain in enrollment. Do not have a high attendance day every week. When you have one, set it on a day when more people normally attend—Mother's Day or Easter, for example. Then when goals are achieved, celebrate the results.

RECLAIMING ABSENTEES

Dealing with chronic absentees is a universal problem in Sunday Schools. In most classes and departments 40 to 50 percent of the members could be classified as chronic absentees. To attempt to reclaim these absentees for regular involvement and participation, consider this thirteen-week contact program.

First, make a list of all Sunday School members, by class, who have not attended in at least three months. Make both a master list and lists by classes.

Second, distribute the class lists to the faithful attenders.

Third, pray for these absentees by name for four weeks.

Fourth, select three faithful members in each class to contact these chronic absentees. When the absentee begins to attend, stop the concentrated contact.

That is an overview of the program. Now let's look at it in more detail.

What we have discovered through testing this program in many churches is that most persons are chronically absent from Sunday School because they have a broken relationship with a Sunday

School teacher or someone in the class. Contacts will not mend these relationships, but prayer can change attitudes. So for the first four weeks, the focus of the program is prayer for the absentees by name. All regular attenders are asked to participate in the prayer. Through the prayer God is preparing the hearts of the absentees to be receptive to the contacts to follow. He is also working in the minds and hearts of those who will make the contacts.

After four weeks of prayer, it is time for the contacts to begin. For the next three weeks, a person we will call Contacter #1, a faithful class member, will concentrate on one or more absentees. The first week a letter is written; the second week a visit is made; and the third week the contact is by telephone.

At that time, Contacter #1 turns his or her names over to Contacter 2, another faithful member of the class. Contacter 2 follows the same process for three weeks and turns his or her names over to Contacter #3, who repeats the process.

As the contacts are made, accurate records must be maintained as to who is making them and how. Responses are noted. As mentioned earlier, whenever an absentee begins to attend, the concentrated contacts are stopped, but efforts are continued to strengthen relationships and to meet needs.

The success of this program is the prayer and the variety of contacts. At least three people are involved, making at least nine different contacts in a three-month period. Through these contacts, reasons are often discovered as to why a person quit attending Sunday School. Sometimes actions can be taken to deal with the problem. In other instances, if the contacter can listen to the problem with compassion and relate to the person in love, the person's attitude may be changed and he or she may experience a change of heart. Through these concentrated contacts needs may be discovered that will result in ministry from the Sunday School class.

People need attention, expressions of concern, a listening ear, and love. Through this program of concentrated contacts, absentees may be reclaimed who can experience growth in their spiritual lives through once again participating in weekly Bible study. They also will have contributions to make which will result in the growth of others.

8

Specific Plan

Between 1970 and 1972 when I began experimenting with the concept of open enrollment, later called ACTION, my purpose was to increase the attendance in Sunday School. After trying many things I concluded that the way to increase attendance in Sunday School is to increase the enrollment. In my own church and others I had observed, I had seen open enrollment consistently accomplish the purpose of increasing attendance through increasing enrollment. However, after beginning work as a consultant at the Sunday School Board in 1975 and working with churches throughout the nation, I began seeing that some churches were implementing ACTION but were not seeing corresponding increases in attendance. I began to ask questions.

Question: How many new persons did you enroll through ACTION?

Answer: 100.

Question: How many new Sunday School classes did you start?

Answer: Were we supposed to start new classes?

Question: How many additional Sunday School workers did you enlist, train, and put to work meeting the needs of a larger enrollment?

Answer: None.

What became evident in the churches where open enrollment did not lead to an increase in attendance was that leaders did not know what to do when growth occurred. They did not know how to *assimilate* the persons being enrolled in the Sunday School and coming into the church. My overriding concern then became how to help churches reach people and integrate them into the community of believers to become active, growing disciples of Christ.

My wife and I have a small cattle ranch in South Florida where we have lived more than a decade. About one hundred yards from the house is a small fish pond. On the bank of that pond is a log where I often sit, fishing pole in hand, and think. I call this my "dia-log" because this is where the Lord and I have many conversations. I shared with Him my concern about helping churches know what to do when growth occurred. "Lord," I prayed, "Some of our people don't know how to minister to the new people they are receiving into their churches. Please help." And He did.

I remained convinced that open enrollment was a viable, valuable tool for reaching people. I also knew the old formula for Sunday School growth created by Arthur Flake—know the possibilities, enlarge the organization, enlist and train the workers, provide the space, and go after the people—had worked in thousands of churches. Every Sunday School that I had studied had grown on that basis. Open enrollment helps churches reach people. The Flake Formula helps Sunday Schools grow. Therefore, while I was sitting on that log by the fish pond, God led me to marry the open enrollment concept to the Flake Formula. The result, over a nine-month period of prayer and fasting, was the Sunday School Growth Spiral (see p. 116).

Before looking at the individual elements of the spiral, I want to outline the overall concept in more detail.

First of all, the Growth Spiral is designed to produce *synchronized growth* or balanced growth. Many times we see churches grow rapidly and then decline almost as quickly. Often the reason is that the Sunday School increases rapidly in enrollment but lacks sufficient teaching units and workers to minister to those who are being enrolled. Other churches may bring in large numbers of people through revivals and evangelistic emphases. However, they may fail to integrate the new converts into the fellowship; and almost as many exit the back door as are entering the front door.

Anything that is grown out of balance will fall. Some churches grow in quantity, but they do not match it with quality and ministry. These churches will not remain strong. Other churches grow in quality and do not balance it with numerical growth. These churches will fall. We must balance three things—quality, quantity, and ministry. The Growth Spiral is designed to balance quantity, quality, and ministry to result in synchronized growth. This is the teaching of the New Testament and should be the practice of our churches.

Second, the Growth Spiral is a *controlled growth process*. Churches are grown on a continuing basis through process, not programs. The control dimension can eliminate the problem of churches enrolling more people than they are equipped to minister to. However, control does not mean thwarting or reducing growth. Growth, no matter how rapid, can be controlled. When growth is controlled, it can be conserved. Most of us have witnessed on television the total destruction of large buildings surrounded by other structures. Through a carefully controlled plan, the building explodes and falls in on itself without damaging the buildings around it. The explosion was controlled. In like manner, a church growth explosion can be controlled so that people are reached and the church expands to accommodate the growth.

Third, the Growth Spiral is an *evaluation tool*. Using the spiral, leaders can evaluate every facet of the Sunday School—space, workers, training, outreach, offerings, attendance, enrollment, baptisms. Formulas can be applied to many of these areas to ensure accurate evaluation. Leaders can locate the weaknesses in the church and make plans to correct them. Strengths can be identified, rejoiced about, and used to help overcome the weaknesses.

Fourth, the Growth Spiral is a *planning tool*. The spiral is a visual method to assist in planning the entire church program. Goals can be projected and progress measured weekly, monthly, and quarterly.

Fifth, the Growth Spiral is a *goal-setting tool*. Setting goals is an art. With the spiral leaders can evaluate their Sunday School and then set enrollment goals and goals for new units, workers, etc. to support the growth. Long-range goals can be established and then broken down into quarterly, monthly, and weekly segments.

Sixth, the spiral is an *administrative tool*. When the goals have been set and plans developed to reach the goals, someone is needed to measure the progress and keep people informed of progress toward attaining the goals. Where weaknesses develop, plans can be implemented to strengthen them. Some ministers of education have chosen to use the Growth Spiral exclusively as an administrative tool. They don't unveil the spiral to the total membership, believing that most persons are not interested in the details of number of prospects, teaching units, workers, etc. However, they monitor all of these very closely. In these instances, the spiral is an administrative tool. Others who keep every facet of progress on the spiral before the people are using it also as an educational and motivational tool.

EVALUATION AND THE GROWTH SPIRAL

The Growth Spiral can be a tool for evaluating the present status of many facets of a church's program. On the basis of that evaluation, goals can be established and strategies developed and implemented for reaching the goals. Then progress toward attaining the goals needs to be evaluated on a regular basis and the goals and strategies readjusted in light of the evaluation. The Growth Spiral is a tool for evaluation. Here's how it works.

First, notice that the Spiral has four quadrants: (1) quantity, (2) quality, (3) outreach/ministry, (4) projections. In each quadrant are categories which, if careful attention is given to each, will result in attaining that dimension of the quadrant. For example, the number of persons enrolled in Sunday School and the number of prospects relate to *quantity,* while *quality* dimensions include units, workers, participation in weekly workers' meeting, and training awards. Evaluate the present status of your Sunday School as follows.

Quantity

1. *Enrollment*—Is the enrollment in your Sunday School larger than it was twelve months ago? If so, place a plus above enrollment. If the enrollment is the same or smaller, place a minus above enrollment.

2. *Prospects*—To be in a position to grow, a Sunday School needs a number of prospects equal to the Sunday School enrollment. Do you have the names, addresses, and telephone numbers of as many prospects as you have people enrolled? If so, give yourself a plus; if not, a minus.

Quality

3. *Teaching Units*—A Sunday School needs an average of one teaching unit for approximately each eighteen members. The exact ratio is determined by adding the number of Preschool and Children's departments to the number of Youth and Adult classes. That figure is the number of teaching units. This should then be divided into the Sunday School enrollment to get the ratio of units to enrollment. If the ratio is 1:18 or less give yourself a plus; if it is 1:19 or more, a minus.

4. *Workers*—A ratio of no more than one worker for each eight members is needed for the kind of ministry to take place that will result in growth. Total the number of workers in the Sunday School and divide this into the Sunday School enrollment. If the ratio is 1:8 or less, mark a plus beside workers on the spiral. If the ratio is 1:9 or more, indicate this with a minus.

5. *Weekly Workers' Meeting*—To attain a plus in this category a Sunday School must have a weekly workers' meeting and then have an average attendance of at least 75 percent of the Sunday School workers. This is necessary because planning cannot take place without most of the workers present. Planning is a vital key to growth.

6. *Training Awards*—An indicator that adequate training is taking place occurs when the number of quarterly training awards equals at least one-half the number of workers. If this is happening on a higher average than the previous year, give yourself a plus. Frequently, on an initial evaluation, this category is one of the greatest weaknesses in the Sunday School. Priority attention needs to be given to continual training efforts in a growing Sunday School.

Outreach/Ministry

7. *Space*—To get a plus in this category, a Sunday School simply needs more space than is presently being utilized for classes and departments. This means new units can be created to enhance the possibilities for growth.

8. *Contacts*—The rule of thumb for contacts is that the number of weekly contacts should equal one-half the Sunday School enroll-

ment. A church with an enrollment of 180 needs a minimum of 90 weekly contacts. If this minimum is being attained, give yourself a plus.

9. *Outreachers*—The number of persons participating in weekly visitation should equal the number of teaching units. For example, a Sunday School with one Preschool department, two Children's departments, one Youth class, and three Adult classes should have an average of at least seven persons participating in weekly visitation. If this average is being reached, give yourself a plus.

Projections

10. *Sunday School Attendance*—Figure the average percentages of enrollment in attendance by dividing the enrollment into the average attendance. If the percentage is between 40 and 60, give yourself a plus. If it is below 40, give yourself a minus. If it is above 60, give yourself a minus unless you are a new church. If the percentage is below 40, look at the categories where you have received minuses. These represent your problems and the factors contributing to a low attendance.

If the average attendance is more than 60 and you are not a new church, chances are good that the Sunday School rolls are being cleaned regularly—that is, persons who do not attend are being dropped. When people are being erased from the rolls instead of becoming objects of ministry, a church will not grow in quality or quantity because there is no concern for lost and hurting people.

At this point, people frequently ask why we have to settle for an average attendance of roughly one-half the enrollment. On a given Sunday, if you add the persons who are out of town, those who are ill, family members of the sick who are caring for them, people who are working and those who are backsliders, chances are good that the total will be close to 50 percent of the enrollment.

11. *Worship Service Attendance*—This is a subjective figure. If you generally feel good about the attendance in worship, give yourself a plus. If not, indicate with a minus. If the worship attendance is substantially lower than the Sunday School attendance, a hard look should be taken at the factors contributing to this.

12. *Budget*—Determine the average individual weekly contributors by dividing the average Sunday School attendance into the

average weekly offerings. This becomes a handle for evaluation as growth occurs. However, for the initial evaluation, give yourself a plus if income allows all the bills to be paid.

13. *Baptisms*—Evaluate baptisms only the first time. After that, if adequate attention is given to all other categories, all factors will be in place to allow God to work in the lives of lost people and baptisms will follow. For the first time, give yourself a plus if you feel a reasonably good job is being done in the area of winning the lost to Christ. This always could and should be better than it is.

Now, review the evaluation and add the total of pluses and minuses. With this evaluation, strengths and weaknesses have been identified. Goals can be established in every area, especially the weaknesses. Areas of strength become resources for dealing with the weaknesses. *The overall goal should be to increase enrollment while changing every minus to a plus within one year.* This means that even as enrollment increases, workers must be enlisted to reach a ratio of 1:8 and units started to attain a ratio of 1:18. The only potential problem area for changing all minuses to pluses in one year may be space.

If growth occurs with the spiral, not only will more people be enrolled in Sunday School, but the quality of Christian education taking place will also be improved. Since the Sunday School belongs to the Lord, we want it to be the best it can possibly be. Having identified our weaknesses, we are ready to undertake the efforts to change the minuses to pluses. As this happens, the result is synchronized, balanced growth.

SETTING GOALS WITH THE GROWTH SPIRAL

To understand the process of setting goals with the Growth Spiral, it is important to contrast the differences between the traditional growth process and the spiral growth process.

In the traditional growth process, leaders of a church take stock of their situation, discover the church has not grown, and make a commitment to growth. Plans are developed and implemented. Growth begins to happen and, within a short period of time, it ceases because the church runs out of space. Leaders determine to build to meet space needs; studies are conducted; plans are developed; construction takes place. Furnishings are purchased, workers enlisted, and new units organized. Finally, the building can be occupied and growth can begin again. However, months or even years have elapsed since the first growth spurt stopped due to lack of space.

Contrast this traditional process with the spiral process.

A church begins at the same place—realizing it has not grown— and workers make a commitment to reaching people. When this decision is made, statistics are reviewed and placed on the spiral. Needs are identified and plans developed to meet those needs. Projections are developed. At the same time, feasibility studies begin, forecasts are conducted, planning and design of needed space is undertaken, and construction is begun. Ideally, the church will never run out of space again because growth is planned along with strategies to accommodate the growth.

Without the Growth Spiral, this kind of planning is difficult. But with the spiral, a church can project the number of classes, the number of square feet needed to accommodate increasing enrollment, and attendance for both Sunday School and worship. Because offerings also can be projected, it is possible to know how much money will be available for construction. The spiral process is, therefore, an invaluable tool for growth. It is a process for using the basics of good Sunday School principles to reach people and teach the Bible in a way that changes lives.

The Growth Spiral is also a process for eliminating the likelihood that leaders could be fooled into believing their church is growing when, in fact, it is declining or standing still.

False growth may take at least four forms.

The first is financial growth. An increase in finances, if not properly understood, can be a false indicator of growth. Some leaders are satisfied if the income of the church keeps pace with the budget. However, in many instances, this increase is only inflationary income. As the salaries of church members increase, their tithes and offerings also increase.

These gains are consumed by the higher cost of operating the church. No actual growth is taking place. For example, one church had a Sunday School enrollment of 1,650 with an average attendance of 813 and an annual income of $350,000. Five years later, the income of the church is $450,000 with a Sunday School enrollment of 1,327 and an average attendance of 704. The church's net increase in income is $100,000.

When this figure is divided by the cost of living increase for the five-year period, we discover that the income of the church is actually declining. And yet when I talked with persons in the church, they spoke of the growth, based on increasing finances. No mention was made of the decline in Sunday School enrollment or attendance. The increase in income represented growth to these church leaders, but this was false growth.

A second form of false growth is biological baptisms. Biological baptisms, conversions of children of church members, often account for the majority of baptisms in a church. Baptizing our children is good practice. It is biblical. But if a church's only baptisms come from this method, the church is not fulfilling the Great Commission. It doesn't require a lot of spiritual power or aggressive outreach and witnessing to lead these children to Christ. To evaluate how well your church is doing in winning the lost, fill in the blanks below.

1. Total baptisms last year: _____
2. Subtract biological baptisms: _____
3. Subtract rebaptisms: _____
    TOTAL—number outside the church
    baptized on initial profession of faith: _____

It takes the full power of God in the lives of church members to win hard-core sinners to Christ. A church that is really growing is reaching people who are outside the church.

Building growth is a third form of false growth. I once conducted a survey for a church that was in the process of building a new worship center. I asked the pastor why they were building an auditorium twice the size of their present facility that would seat four times the Sunday School attendance in spite of the fact that a lack of educational space was a barrier to growth. The pastor's response to my question was, "When you stop growing numerically, you have to keep something going. We chose to do this." The survey I completed for the church showed a decline in Sunday School enrollment, Sunday School attendance, worship service attendance, and baptisms. Four years after I completed the survey I went by the church again. The attendance was smaller; the indebtedness was larger; dissatisfaction reigned among the people;

and the pastor had resigned. Building growth can be false growth.

 A large number of baptisms which are not accompanied by a corresponding increase in Sunday School enrollment and attendance is a fourth form of false growth. Let me illustrate. I have a pastor-friend who is very evangelistic. He schedules two revivals a year in the church he has served more than twenty years. The church baptizes between 100 and 200 converts each year. On the basis of this figure, the church appears to be growing in an outstanding way. But look again.

When I met this pastor twenty years ago, the Sunday School enrollment in the church was approximately 550. Twenty years later it has grown to 800. However, more than 2,500 persons have been baptized into the fellowship of the church during these years. Perhaps just as many have been received by transfer of membership.

The problem in this church is that the back door of the church is almost as large as the front door. Failing to enroll these new church members in Sunday School and to disciple them has caused the church to lose them. Winning and baptizing is only the beginning. The church is also charged with teaching these new Christians.

The Growth Spiral is not an automatic solution to eliminate false growth. However, the use of the spiral will enable a church to spot problems that may be creating false impressions of growth and develop strategies to strengthen weaknesses and eliminate problems. The result is balanced growth in all areas of church programming.

CONTROLLING AND PROJECTING GROWTH

The items on the Growth Spiral are the factors which produce numerical growth in a church. All of these are controllables. For example, leaders can control the enrollment. They can clean the roll and reduce the enrollment or reach more persons and increase the enrollment. In the same way, the number of teaching units can be controlled by combining classes and reducing the number of units or starting new classes and increasing the number.

The number of workers also can be controlled. Workers can be dismissed or new workers enlisted and trained to increase the number. The motivation and training of workers also can be controlled. Sunday School leaders determine whether a weekly workers' meeting will be held. If there is none, the planning, motivating, and the training of the workers goes lacking. Space also is controlled by leaders; it can be used once, twice, or three times on Sunday morning. The priority given to contacts and weekly outreach by the leaders is also a controlling factor in these areas.

Sunday School leaders control all of these factors which produce numerical growth. Therefore, the leaders decide in advance whether the church will grow during the next year. No church grows accidentally; no church declines accidentally. The Growth Spiral then can be a tool for projecting growth.

The laws or basics of growth through the Sunday School have been outlined on the pages of this book. When we apply these laws, we cause growth to happen and we can project the results. For example, if we do *not* increase the enrollment of the Sunday School, create additional teaching units, enlist or train additional workers, contact, visit, or minister, there will be *no* additional growth in the church next year. However, if we *do* increase the enrollment, number of units, enlist and train more workers, visit, contact, and minister, then there *will* be additional growth. As we increase the enrollment, if we build in the same quality that we have at this time, then we can expect the same results.

Southern Baptists have embarked upon what I believe is a God-given mission in Bold Mission Thrust, a worldwide effort to share the gospel with every person in the world by the year 2000. Bold Mission Thrust is the most aggressive, daring outreach concept ever undertaken by Southern Baptists. However, as I travel from place to place, I find few, if any, churches which have bold goals. In conferences I lead I often attempt to get people's attention and make them think about their own situation by saying what I believe to be true—that I do not recall having seen many goals that could not be reached even if God were dead. I do not mean this sacrilegiously. I am simply saying that in many churches the goals are so small that they could be achieved with human effort alone.

What is needed in today's world with more than 120 million lost people in the United States alone is faith goals. We need to launch out into fields of activity and growth that we have never dreamed possible. A faith goal is one that would require the best combined efforts of all church members under the leadership of the Holy Spirit.

As a takeoff from Bold Mission Thrust, which I believe in and support totally, I have developed what I call a "Timid Mission Thrust."

The Southern Baptist Convention is made up of approximately 36,000 churches. If each church registered a *net* Sunday School enrollment increase of two people per week, the denomination would experience a Sunday School enrollment increase of more than 70,000 per week. The result sounds impressive, but I do not believe that a net Sunday School enrollment increase of two per week per church is a bold goal. It is rather timid. This does not include increasing the attendance by two each week or baptizing two per week. This is simply a goal of enrolling a net gain of two persons per week in Sunday School.

If this were continued for 52 weeks, Southern Baptists would see a net enrollment increase of 3,754,000. In five years, this Timid Mission Thrust would bring about a net increase in the Southern Baptist Sunday School enrollment of 18.7 million, bringing the total Sunday School enrollment to more than 27 million.

If the ratio of unsaved persons remained approximately the same, more than 10 million lost people would be enrolled in Southern Baptist Sunday Schools in five years. It is reasonable to expect that five million of these would be baptized within one year of their being enrolled in Sunday School. Through Timid Mission Thrust, the average attendance in Bible study on Sunday mornings would top 13 million.

This is the kind of growth that can be projected among 36,000 churches using the spiral process and the Growth Spiral as a *tool*. However, these are only imaginary figures on paper until leaders of individual churches determine, through the leadership of the Holy Spirit, to dare to catch a vision, set bold goals, and develop and implement strategies to reach the goals. Whatever the goal, the Growth Spiral represents a process for using the basic principles of growth through the Sunday School to reach people for Jesus Christ, to minister to them in His name, and to enable them to grow as His disciples.

I believe every church can grow. Every church should grow if its leaders accept the truth of the Great Commission and embark upon the exciting, challenging journey of reaching, teaching, and discipling.

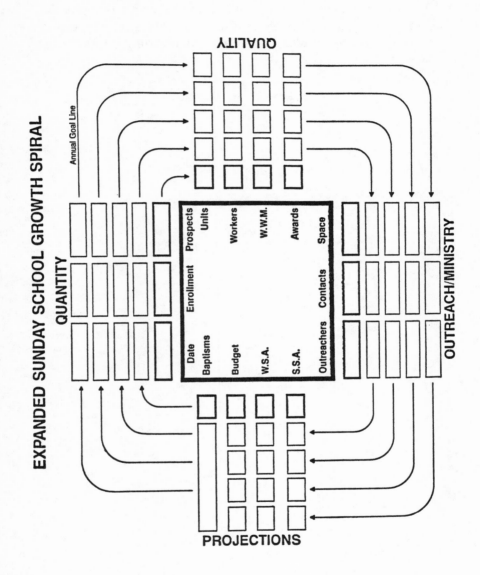

EXPANDED SUNDAY SCHOOL GROWTH SPIRAL

QUALITY

QUANTITY

OUTREACH/MINISTRY

PROJECTIONS

Annual Goal Line

Date
Baptisms
Enrollment
Prospects
Units
Budget
Workers
W.S.A.
W.W.M.
S.S.A.
Awards
Outreachers
Contacts
Space

GROWTH SPIRAL

1. Syncronized Growth

2. Controlled Growth Process

3. Evaluation Tool

4. Planning Tool

5. Goal Setting Tool

6. Administration Tool

Church _____ Pastor _____

Address _____ M. E. _____

Phone ( ) _____

Growth Spiral QUARTERLY REVIEW

FIVE YEAR REVIEW BEFORE ENTERING SPIRAL

	SS Enr.	SS Att.	Budget Inc.	Baptisms
19_				
19_				
19_				
19_				
19_				

	Start Date	1st Qtr.		2nd Qtr.		3rd Qtr.		4th Qtr.		1st Qtr.		2nd Qtr.		3rd Qtr.		4th Qtr.	
	Actual	Date Goal	Actual	Date Goal	Actual	Date Goal	Actual	Date Goal	Actual	Date Goal	Actual	Date Goal	Actual	Date Goal	Actual	Date Goal	Actual
Enrollment																	
Prospects																	
Units																	
Workers																	
W. W. M.																	
Awards																	
Space																	
Contacts																	
Outreachers																	
S. S. Att.																	
W. S. Att.																	
Budget																	
Baptisms																	
New S. S.'s																	

TRADITIONAL GROWTH PROCESS

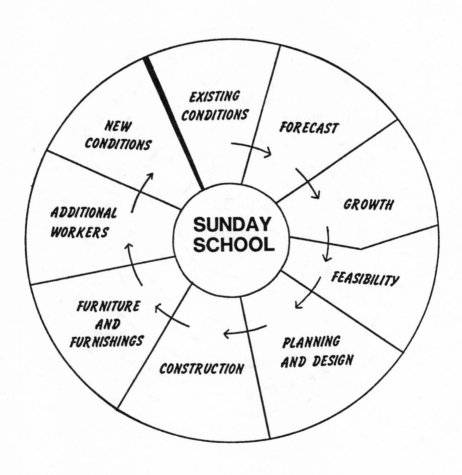

SPIRAL GROWTH PROCESS

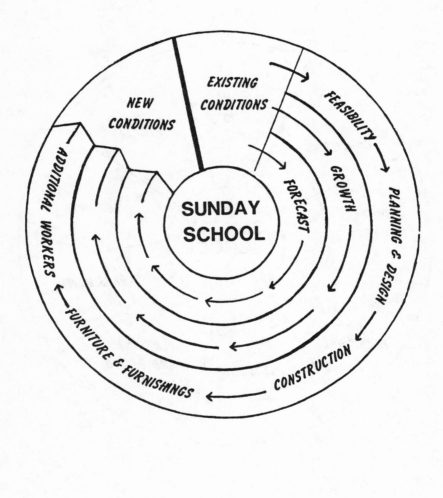